How to Speak Furniture with an Antique French Accent

Formal and Regional Furniture Charts
Clues, Clarifications, History, and
Characteristics
Buying-Selling-Auction Advice

Jeanne Siegel

Bonus Books, Inc., Chicago

98 97 96 95 94   5 4 3 2 1

Library of Congress Catalog Card Number: 93-074132

International Standard Book Number: 1-56625-003-X

Bonus Books, Inc.
160 East Illinois Street
Chicago, Illinois 60611

All insert illustrations by Jeanne Siegel

Cover photo courtesy of Antique Emporium

Composition by Point West, Inc., Carol Stream, IL

Printed in the United States of America

This book is dedicated to French furniture
always enchanting
always in good taste

and mère Florence

CONTENTS

ACKNOWLEDGEMENTS

Louvre Museum
du Musée des Arts Decoratifs
Service, Photographique
Paris, France
Thank you to Véronique Bourvet for photographs.

William Doyle Galleries
175 East 87th Street
New York, New York
Thank you to Diane Whiteley for great photographs.

The Antique Emporium
915 Green Bay Road
Winnetka, Illinois

Leslie Hindman Auctioneers
215 West Ohio Street
Chicago, Illinois
Thank you to Maron Matz for photographs.

Victoria & Albert Museum, London, England.

Proofread by Julie B. Halpern, New York.

Again many thanks, times four, to Claudette Giss for her invaluable
typing of this manuscript.

WHY THIS BOOK?

This book is proof that a room can open a door.

It happened at my second cousin's daughter's eighth birthday party. We were going out to see a movie, but first everyone assembled in my cousin Celia's living room. It was the prettiest room I had ever seen. As I remember, the furniture was painted, curvy, cushioned, and everything was blue or pink. I couldn't believe my eyes. A pink and blue living room (blue walls, pastel silk upholsterings, and shimmering opalines). I have no recollection of the movie, except that we sat in the balcony; but I still experience pleasure when I enter a French room.

Years later I discovered that that enchanting room was decorated with French pieces. I have no idea if the furniture was "antique," "in the style of," or merely "reproduction." It doesn't really matter. I had fallen under the spell of French design.

When I grew up I became an interior contents appaiser. I studied many styles of furniture and enjoy them all. When clients ask: "What is a good buy?" I always reply: "Only what invariably draws your eyes." Those things will be the happiest investments of your life. If French furniture holds your eyes and heart, this book is for you.

I have previously written books dealing with wonderful American, Victorian, and English furniture, all with similar furniture characteristics, and all sharing French influences. I have used research from these books when it applied to this work. I want my books to provide information about furniture periods, styles, and easy recognition. The descriptive words aid in identifying furniture and impart the flavor of the pieces.

Vocabulary is a must. If you know the right words, their meanings and sounds, you will enjoy furniture more fully. I urge you to read a few words each day, and soon you will be caught up in the language of French furniture. This is the world of taupie feet, chutes, sabots, fauteuils and ébénistes.

This book studies the major French furniture periods beginning in the Middle Ages. It also parallels Paris styles with seventeenth, eighteenth, and nineteenth century regional pieces known as provincial furniture. I include an eighteenth century map of these provinces. Photographs and drawings indicate designs and styles of these eighteenth century pieces.

I tucked in French "Petit Points" to provide historical background and a little fun, a chapter entitled "Clues, Characteristics, and Chicanery" to save you from costly mistakes, and another chapter on auctions. I include a chronology of the monarchs and the characteristics of their times for quick reference.

I believe it is possible to collect and to furnish with French furniture for the price of fine new furniture. French furniture presents different problems and approaches from collecting antique furniture in general. These methods are discussed in the chapters on "Collecting and Buying," "Clarifications," and "Price Guides."

Perhaps someday another child will open a door and say "This is the prettiest room I ever saw." It could be a small visitor, a beloved grandchild, or even the child within yourself.

CHRONOLOGY OF FRENCH RULERS FROM LOUIS VII TO NAPOLEON III AND PERIOD FURNITURE DESIGNS

Louis VII 1137–1180
m. Eleanor of Aquitaine

Philip Augustus II 1180–1123
m. Isabella of Hainaut

Louis VIII 1223–1226
m. Blanche of Castile

Louis IX (Saint Louis) 1226–1270
m. Margaret of Provence

Philip III 1270–1285
m. Mary Brabant

Philip IV 1285–1314
m. Joan of Navarre

The Sons of Philip 1314–1328

Philip VI 1328–1350

John II 1350–1364

Charles V 1364–1380

Charles VI 1380–1422
m. Isabeau of Bavaria

Charles II 1422–1461
m. Mary of Anjou

Middle Ages
Romanesque and subsequently
Gothic designs. Simplicity,
arch designs, iron fittings,
linenfold carving.

Louis XI 1461–1483
m. Charlotte of Savoy

Charles VIII 1483–1498
m. Anne of Britanny

Louis XII 1498–1515
m. Anne of Brittany, widow
of Charles VIII

Renaissance influence
The Italian Renaissance
influence reaches France. This
is a transitional period.
Geometric and floral motifs.

Francis I 1515–1547
m. Claude of France and
Eleanor of Austria

The Renaissance influence
continues. Grotesques, fantasy
fauna, cartouches, human
figures incorporated, pilasters,
large turnings. Francis I style
called "First Renaissance."

Henry II 1547–1559
m. Catherine de Médici

Classical designs. Knob, bun,
animal feet, balusters, caryatids,
monsters, human figures,
acanthus motifs, and broken
pediments. Henry II style called
"High Renaissance."

Francis II 1559–1560
m. Mary Stuart

Charles IX 1560–1574

Henry III 1574–1589

Henry IV 1589–1610
m. Margaret of Valois
and Maria de Medici

Installed artisans in the Louvre
galleries. Italian, Spanish and
Dutch influences.

Louis XIII 1610–1643
m. Anne of Austria

Transitional period. Italian
Renaissance designs combined

with other foreign influence.
Garlands, fruit clusters, thick
foliage, veneering.

Louis XIV 1643–1715 m. Maria Theresa	Genuine French style emerges. Interior decoration viewed as an ensemble. Veneering, marquetry, bronze mounts.
Régence 1715–1723	Louis XIV designs continue. Symmetry.
Louis XV 1715–1774 m. Maria Leczinska	Golden Age of French furniture. Marquetry, chinoiserie, lacquering, bronze mounts, rococo designs.
Louis XVI 1774–1793 m. Marie Antoinette	A return towards antiquity. Marquetry, veneering, porcelain and Wedgewood plaques. Brass strips, pierced galleries, Greek-key motif.

Directoire 1795–1799	Louis XVI styles continued. Classical Greek style important.
Napoleon 1799 in power Napòleon 1803 Emperor Napoleon 1814 abdicated	Empire style. Monumental pieces, veneering, inlay, bronze mounts, Motifs of bees, wreaths, classical drapery, terminal busts, military.

Louis XVIII 1814–1824 (Restoration)	Empire designs and revivals from Gothic to Louis XVI

Charles X 1824–1830	Neo-Gothic, Neo-Egyptian, Oriental influence. Rosettes, quatrefoils, pale woods.
Louis-Philippe I 1830–1848 m. Marie-Amelie	Dark woods, heavy pieces, broad cornices, industrial production. Similar to Restoration pieces.
Second Republic 1848–1852	Industrialization continued. Large pieces, hard contours.
Napoleon III 1852–1870 Emperor m. Eugénie	Called Second Empire. Revival furniture. Highly decorated. In part paralleled English Victorian period.

INTRODUCTION TO FRENCH FURNITURE

What does the word "French" conjure up? French dressing, French fashion, French kisses, French accents, and perhaps French porcelain, Napoleon and lots of Louies. If asked to describe French furniture, nine out of ten people would probably answer, "fancy carved" or "French provincial." Most forget that French families had domestic furniture from various periods and in many styles. In each of these periods, whether from city or town, the grace and exquisite taste of French furniture is evident.

The name "France" did not appear until the tenth century when the great nobles conferred on one of their number the title of "King of the Ile de France," the term covering Paris itself and the collection of counties and provinces in its immediate neighborhood. What is referred to as French furniture began in the Middle Ages with Gothic designs. When the Italian Renaissance reached France, the French nobility desired this beauty for themselves. First they imported Italian furniture. Then they imported Italian craftsmen as teachers. Influences from Germany, Holland, Belgium and Spain were absorbed into an emerging French national style. Although French furniture owes great debt to Italian design, ultimately France created superb unique furniture.

During the seventeenth century, the student surpassed the master. French court pieces are probably the most glorious, and the most exquisitely crafted furniture man ever created! They are a visual delight and have masterpiece construction.

Furniture from the provinces reflected these court designs in a simplified form, combining them with local woods and unique neighborhood characteristics. The individuality of the local craftsman is evident in provincial furniture in contrast to that of court furniture made collectively by the guilds.

French furniture ranges in variety to suit a palace, a penthouse, a country house, or your home. I am writing this book on my provincial dining room table in our 1950 tri-level house.

With the exception of our English heritage, the French influence in culture, fashion, food and philosophy has been the strongest legacy in America's history.

French furniture, whether found in the elegant salons of Paris or the poorest Basque or Limousin towns, fascinates furniture lovers throughout the world. These designs, originally meant for kings, bring enchantment to our lives.

Benjamin Franklin said, and I quote, "Every civilized man has two homelands, and one of them is France."

CLARIFICATIONS FOR THE COLLECTOR

We are collecting antique French furniture, so we ask: "Is the piece French? Are we sure?"

Authentic furniture has its origin supported by unquestionable evidence.

A reproduction or replica is a copy. With a little help it might be sold as an authentic piece.

A fake is a copy of an authentic piece made to be sold as if it were the "real thing." "Nice people" sell "unnice" pieces.

What is the approximate date that the piece was made? Is that date the period that it actually belongs to? A very important point. Is it "of the period?"

Has it been altered? Is this fine commode really a gussied-up chest?

Can I see any visible age, soft edges, wear, cracks, or repairs? If not, I doubt its age.

Repair: This term refers to small mending, not substituting or adding new parts to any degree.

Restoration is more than simple repair. It means to renew and return a piece to its first state. New parts can be substituted for missing or damaged ones. *Restoration is proper and important.* Without restoration, many lovely pieces would be lost forever. Skilled craftspeople are very valuable. Major restorations include the replacement of front legs, feet, casepiece tops, or one or more drawers, and reshaping a seat frame, a chair back, or the wings of an armchair. Expert workmanship is very important.

Natural patina is a mellow quality that furniture surfaces acquire with age. This is why refinishing, stripping, or French polishing injures antique pieces.

Unnatural patina is a wood surface showing refinishing, French polishing, or other unnatural devices such as fake insect evidence.

The more you handle antique furniture, touch it, measure

3

it with your eyes, rub your fingers over it, and mentally compare it with similar pieces, the quicker you will develop instinct. Instinct is important! You will appreciate the beauty of old walnut patinas, notice the soft edges on true antique pieces, and feel the "cold velvet" of old marble. If I see "harsh tones," "sharp edges," or "yogurt" instead of "cold velvet," I back off.

A provenance is a written history or pedigree of a piece: who made it, where it was made, who originally owned it, when it was last sold, and so on.

Ask for a written description of your purchase on the shop letterhead, including the price. This is also important if the piece is stolen, broken by a moving company, or damaged in a fire. Your heirs will also appreciate this.

What is a proper description? Example: "A fine Louis XV marquetry bureau plat. Circa 1765. The shaped serpentine top inset with brown leather and with a molded gilt-bronze border. The shaped frieze set with conforming end-cut marquetry panels. Three drawers on one side. Cabriole legs. Well-cast gilt-bronze mounts. Amaranth and Tulipwood. Two feet, six inches high; three feet, nine inches wide; two feet, two and a half inches deep."

Appreciate dealers with fine, very deserved reputations who have remained in business for many years. If an honest mistake is made or if you want to upgrade or sell back, these dealers will try to oblige. They are usually delighted to get one of their earlier pieces returned.

If a piece is in the thousands, a carved fauteuil or commode with bronze-gilt mounts, consider an hour of an appraiser's time.

The collector looks for what is beautiful. The appraiser must look first for what is wrong. If we find too many "wrongs," we may not consider a piece beautiful.

An appraisal is the worth of a piece, valued by an expert, usually in writing, often for insurance.

Market value is the retail cash value of a piece.

"Subbed" is substituting parts, or making a repair or addition, such as gilt bronze mounts, for the purpose of making a piece look older or more valuable.

Antique stool legs that have shorter legs than ordinary chair legs can be employed to construct expensive wing chairs that had short legs. This is why it is preferable to buy an antique frame and have it upholstered.

Most dealers keep a polaroid camera on hand; if so, ask for a picture. If not, photograph your antique furniture yourself. Keep copies in a safe deposit box.

Transitional furniture is furniture with details from two contiguous periods. This is why it is important to know the major periods and the order in which they appear. The latest characteristics on a piece determine its period. An example is seen in the reign of Charles VIII where Gothic and Renaissance designs merged.

I encourage you to frequent auction houses. Viewing is an important "hands-on" learning tool. If you are concerned with the reputation of the auction house, check with an estate lawyer or an appraiser. Auction houses are important to us whether we are the buyer or the seller.

Buying at charity sales may allow you a tax write-off, but if it is not what you really want, you will never enjoy the piece.

Always buy from a shop's owner if possible. An assistant usually cannot negotiate the price lower than ten percent. Often the owner will be more flexible, depending on the original cost to him, how long it has been unsold, or if a loan was required to buy it. It never hurts to bargain.

Painted pieces are becoming more important to the collector. It is important not to strip or repaint these pieces since this will destroy their potential value. These old painted beauties are better left alone.

Decorators have a reputation of marketing quasi-antiques, but don't tar them all with the same brush. Again, whatever you buy, get a written description under a letterhead.

No one fakes an inexpensive piece or a readily available authentic piece. For instance, Napoleon III and Victorian furniture is not scarce, so it is not faked.

Since a set of six or eight antique chairs is more expensive than a set of four, a faker will take four original chairs apart and by making new parts (members), assemble the four into six or eight chairs with intermingled parts.

Faked pieces are more often composed of antique wood fragments than made of new woods.

Are the edges sharp? Old edges have softened. New replacements can be felt by touching.

A faked piece will be "tight," while an antique piece "gives." This is because wood shrinks with age so the joints will be looser.

Old furniture shrinks because wood is eighty to ninety percent water. Round tables are no longer symmetrically round. Drawers may no longer fit perfectly. Inlay shows shrinkage. This is proper.

"All original" is fantastic and probably unrealistic.

Look at furniture you are considering in good light. If possible, take the piece outside. I appraise furniture in daylight, never at night.

Study the entire piece: the legs, bottom, top, sides and back, including the cornice or pediment. Are the proportions correct? Request a ladder if necessary.

Remove every drawer. Check the drawer runners. The inside condition will indicate repairs, remodeling, and any changes.

Ask to have all known repairs pointed out.

If a piece has "in the rough" on it, this means it is in need of repair.

Is the wear in proper places? This is important! Otherwise suspect replacements.

Check feet carefully for damages. Will you have to restore any part of the piece? The price should reflect this.

Early dovetails were not carbon copies of each other. Later dovetails have identical and uniform shapes. Dovetails can be seen in museums on ancient Egyptian pieces proving that if it works, don't change it.

Old dowels, wooden pins, are not uniformly round. Those produced by machines are.

Screws were handmade from the sixteenth century through the latter part of the eighteenth century.

One antique piece can be "twinned" to make two antique pieces. Check both sides of a piece.

Do veneered panels, above and below, match? Do they exhibit the same grain patterns?

Dirty furniture looks older than clean furniture, but old

dirt and wax build-up in crevices and cracks is a good sign. If pristine, look again.

Check to see if castors have been removed. If so, the value is less. Try to replace with period pieces.

Splotches of stain are a warning. Check the area very carefully, inside and out. Has the area been repaired, remodeled, or replaced?

Old newspapers or memorabilia have been known to find their way into new pieces. This is called salting.

Don't be afraid to give a little shake to a chair, étagère, or cabinet. You want solid, not wiggly furniture. If it is loose, will the dealer see to its repair?

There are forged cabinetmaker marks. Remember to look carefully at the piece and judge on merit.

Carry a flashlight and tape measure. Keep a notebook for prices, phone numbers, names, etc.

Layers of beeswax contribute to the look and aroma of antique furniture. Don't allow "antique perfume" to sway your senses.

Living insects eat wood exactly like their ancestors (worm holes). Living forgers also use ice picks and various sizes of nails.

Wood pieces that have dry rot should not be purchased. The microscopic insects could infect your other furniture unless treated by an expert. If you see insect holes, tap the area to determine if it is hollow.

The first piece of a collection is similar to a first romance. You may never be quite the same again.

CLUES, CHARACTERISTICS, AND CHICANERY

All woods involved in furniture making come under the heading "bois d'ébénisterie."

The woods for French furniture were native, such as oak and walnut, or imported, such as ebony or purplewood.

French furniture was made with a great variety of woods. Early pieces were of oak and walnut, but as the Italian Renaissance moved into France, more woods were employed. By the eighteenth century the variety was impressive. The most popular woods were oak, walnut, rosewood, mahogany, beech, tulipwood, ash-burr, holly, yoke-elm, sycamore, violet wood, lemonwood, ebony, lime-wood, boxwood, amaranth, snakewood, satinwood, kingwood, pa-douk wood, casuarina, and hazelwood. Native fruitwoods are often seen on regional pieces.

In the eleventh century, the pointed gothic arch was used in architecture and for furniture design.

Early furniture pieces were simply made by placing planks of wood side by side, and fastening them together with an iron band.

The end of the thirteenth century saw the use of joints. Ultimately, approximately forty types of joints were used on French furniture.

The mortice and tenon joint: two pieces of wood joined together at right angles. The tenon is a projection at the end of one member that is fitted into a corresponding opening called a mortice.

The open tenon joint is where the tenon has the same width as the member of which it forms a part. The result is a shape like fork prongs.

Dowel joints are dowels that consist of small cylinders of wood. These were used for narrow, thin wood pieces. Two or three doweling pins substituted for a tenon. The pins were driven in and then glued.

A concealed joint is employed when the joint is not meant to show on the surface. A thin piece of wood on the outer surface of the joined pieces is left uncut, covering the joint.

The tongue-and-groove joint is used when members have to be joined lengthwise in order to form panels that are wider than the planks available. The tongue is the piece that solves the problem.

The mitre joint unites two members at an angle of forty-five degrees, forming a frame. It is more sophisticated than the square-cut mortice and tenon joint.

Materials such as bronze, silver, ivory, mosaic, brass, marble, cane, and porcelain were used in furniture design and are called secondary materials.

Carving appears on French furniture from the thirteenth century.

The term "supports" usually refers to legs.

All projections—round, square, curved or straight—that decorate a piece are called moldings. Various moldings are flat, curved, combined, plain, or carved. Acanthus leaves, waves, ribbons, fish scales, beading, egg-and-dart, Greek key and interlaced designs, to name a few, decorate various moldings.

Turning is the shaping of wood on a lathe with the help of turning chisels.

Inlay was an early form of decoration. Pieces of the base wood were cut out and new pieces of colored wood or other material were placed in the cavity and glued down. During the Renaissance inlays were made with precious stones, brass, pewter, mother-of-pearl, and bone. Inlay was also laid around marquetry. When inlays are woods, they are cut across the grain.

Marquetry pieces were cut from the wood grain. Marquetry is contrasting inlay. Various materials may be introduced. Marquetry is more complicated than ordinary inlay. It can cover entire surfaces with floral or intricate arabesque designs.

Veneered pieces are achieved by application to the carcass surface. The surface is not chiseled out, but remains flat. The veneer is a separate layer that is applied to the base. The base (carcass) will be a local wood like oak or pine.

Parquetry are small strips, often cut from the same wood and arranged in elaborate geometric patterns that may cover an entire piece. When woods are mixed, a polychrome parquetry is achieved.

Cross-banding is a border that frames a panel, with wood that travels in a different direction than that of the panel and matches at the corners.

France, like most countries, has a long history of painted furniture. Pieces dating from the Middle Ages bear traces of paint. In the seventeenth and eighteenth centuries many chairs and beds were gilded or painted in many colors. Blue, sea-green, and gray were popular. Often, the piece was painted in one color and the molding in another.

The pointed arch may have been introduced into France by the Normans, who had seen them in Sicily.

Early French pieces combine Gothic with Romanesque. Later, French pieces combined Italian Renaissance with Gothic designs.

Many Gothic chests from the Middle Ages may be Flemish, English, or French. They are similar.

Gothic chests for sale are usually whole or partial fakes. Many were made of old wood fragments about 1830 when the Gothic style became fashionable again.

Sixteenth-century coffers were decorated with architectural pilasters that separated the panels.

The equivalent of the medieval French "throne chair" was the medieval English "great chair."

Wrought-iron pierced mounts (hardware), a feature of gothic furniture, were rarely used after the reign of Francis I.

The early French cupboard was called an armoire. The early English cupboard was called an "ambry." The French word "armoire" is still in general use while the word "ambry" is not.

Almost all furniture-makers had to identify their pieces with an iron stamp in keeping with guild regulations. The exceptions were those under royal patronage who were exempt. Unfortunately, stamps can be forged.

The Renaissance saw the introduction of the light armchair with slender elements in contrast to earlier heavy, architectural chairs.

The menuisiers created furniture cut from solid wood often

with carved designs. The ébénistes usually faced the surfaces of furniture with veneers.

There were also "free craftsmen" in Paris who competed with guild members.

The palace at Fontainebleau combined French and Italian craftsmanship and designs. The results are known as Francis I style or First Renaissance (1483–1547).

Italian designers introduced Mannerist sixteenth-century features into France. These features included classical figures, draped or nude, architectural columns, garlands, putti (cherubs), monsters, and grotesques.

Seventeenth- and eighteenth-century rooms usually had their furniture placed against the walls in a formal manner. During the nineteenth century, furniture was designed to stand alone. For example, large ottomans sometimes had sculpture or plants in their raised centers.

The French and the English made a farthingale chair for women wearing a farthingale (hoop). The English chair was open above the seat-back, while the French chair had the back flush against the seat and was taller.

In 1740 the Martin brothers patented "vernis Martin" which was a process to imitate Oriental lacquer.

Use of mahogany on French furniture occured about 1740.

Boulle marquetry appeared in the late seventeenth century.

Rococo designs date from the eighteenth century.

Most provincial pieces were made of solid wood.

The upholsterer, called a tapissier, used silks, velvets, linen, leather and tapestries.

Ancient Oriental furniture elements had a strong influence on French furniture. Examples are: metal mounts, caning, lattice-work, tambour doors, lacquering, and porcelain work.

The technical perfection of French eighteenth-century furniture has never been duplicated. It could not even be duplicated in later French periods.

Many of us would settle for a good forgery of a fine French piece if the price was right.

Rococo designs (Louis XV period) exhibit movement with their sweeping curves, asymmetry of swirls, waves, whorls, leaves, flowers, and scrolls.

From about 1775 (Louis XVI) commodes took a new shape with blunter angles and with their sides widening toward the back.

Gilt bronze is important in eighteenth-century decoration. It was used on furniture, clocks, fire-dogs, chandeliers, and vases. Some beds were made of steel and gilt bronze.

Louis XV furniture has undulating curves (rococo style).

Louis XVI furniture gave way to straighter lines (neo-classic style).

English styles enjoyed a vogue in France between 1785 and the Revolution. Simple pieces with plain mahogany veneers were popular. Today, furniture in "le style Anglais" is still purchased in France.

The mounts on Louis XVI furniture are more delicate at the end of the period.

Mid-eighteenth-century small round tables, often called "work tables," stand on three or four legs with a round lower shelf, a porcelain top, porcelain plaques on the sides, tiers with pierced metal galleries, and legs with gilt bronze decoration.

The earliest types of Sèvres decorated furniture to be produced were small tables with porcelain tray tops.

Riesener married Oeben's widow. He gained the rank of master in 1768. He provided the French court with more than 700 pieces of furniture between 1774 and 1784, as well as supplying a large number of other clients. However, it was for Marie Antoinette that he created his greatest masterpieces.

A French ébéniste would shape the ends of the drawers on a commode to follow the outline of the sides. English cabinet-makers, perhaps, did not have the skill to achieve this, and their commodes have the drawer ends cut off square.

Japanese-lacquered panels, often borrowed from chests or screens, were incorporated into French pieces. Weisweiler used them on armoires and cabinets (circa 1780).

George Jacob was the most famous Parisian menuisier in the Louis XVI court. He survived the Revolution and died naturally in 1814.

Carved fleur de lys are not found on furniture made before the Revolution. Anyone found to possess pieces with this symbol would have been considered the "enemy" and been placed in grave danger. Therefore, people removed this design from any piece they owned. You will not find it on "original" furniture dating before 1789. However, in the Restoration period Louis XVIII removed Napoleon's bees and put back the fleur de lys (1814–1824).

It was during the Régence period that "caned" chairs were most popular. Twin serpent handles were a Régence detail.

The style that succeeded the Revolution is called "le style directoire." It only lasted four years.

Gondola chairs were popular during the Empire period and also after the Restoration.

Popular Empire motifs were bees, N's, eagles, heads of warriors, circles of stars, lances, thunderbolts, and wreaths of ivy; also vines, laurel, and oak leaves interlaced with ribbons.

To determine if an Empire chair is from early in the period, examine the terminal part of the back, which used to curl in an S before becoming straight.

A pianoforte belonging to Queen Hortense (Empire period) was decorated with plaques of verre églomisé, which is painted and gold-inlaid glass.

The Restoration period (1814–1850) was a period of revivals, machine-made furniture, and the comfort that coil-springs could provide. The same could be said of English and American furniture at this time.

Industrial furniture production is evident in the reign of Louis-Philippe I (1830–1848).

In the 1870s, American (Victorian period) "Louis Seize" (Louis XVI) style cabinets were made by cabinetmakers such as Alexander Roux and Leon Marcotte in New York. They were referred to as "French cabinets." These highly decorated pieces have pseudo Ionic capitals, paneling, ornamental brass, porcelain medallions, gilt carvings, and multi-colored inlay, and were made of ebonized rosewood. Owners of these pieces do not always believe me when I say they are American. It is a fact, not an insult. These "French" pieces have high-quality workmanship and are lovely. They just are not French.

PETIT POINTS

The oldest piece of furniture in a French museum comes from the reign of King Dagobert (629–639). It is a gilt-bronze armchair.

Kings give expensive gifts. (Elvis Presley gave Cadillac cars.) Louis XIV gave away beds. His own beds were often decorated with obscene pictures.

Medieval hospitality demanded that the bed be shared with one's guests.

The seigneurs of the Middle Ages lived like rodeo cowboys on the circuit, earning their livelihood by travelling from tournament to tournament, competing for prizes.

In the tenth century, a "chateau" consisted of only a timbered tower perched on a hill, protected by a wall and a moat. This is a far cry from the modern conception of a chateau (beautiful houses complete with turrets, gardens and vineyards).

The first opera whose music has survived was performed in 1600 for the wedding of Henry IV of France to Marie de Médici at the Pitti Palace in Florence.

Eleanor of Aquitaine was a queen of France and also a queen of England. She was married first to Louis VII, and subsequently to Henry II.

The lord and his lady sat separately from family and servants. This was the custom in England also. Only important guests were seated with the master. In England the lord and lady sat on a raised platform, while in France the lord and lady were seated in a specially built stall.

The medieval church at Arles, the church of Saint-Trophime, constructed and carved between 1180 and 1210, has been called a stupendous example of the art of carving. When Vincent Van Gogh saw the church, he called it a "Chinese nightmare."

The Middle Ages were strong on dancing. A curious argument in favor of dancing was that it revealed whether lovers were healthy and, when they kissed, if their breath was sweet.

Louis IX (called Saint Louis) (1226–1270) restricted the streets where prostitutes might live in their bordellos. The women could solicit during the day but had to be indoors by six o'clock.

In 1254 the Provost of Paris ordained that chestmakers should have their own guild and be separate from the carpenters guild.

Prices and standards of workmanship were fixed by the craftsmen themselves through their guilds.

Charles V (1364–1380) owned a set of forks, rare in France, although common in Italy.

In 1392 there were twenty-six public baths in Paris. Mixed bathing was the rule. Bathrobes could be rented. In the sixteenth century they were abolished due to the fear of syphilis.

Thick slices of stale bread were generally used as trenchers (plates) in France and England by all classes of people. Surprisingly, many French peasants actually owned faience plates.

The custom of placing guests at table by couples was introduced in the fourteenth century, each couple having but one cup and one plate. Hence the expression "to eat from the same plate."

Cookbooks appeared in the fourteenth century.

Many French towns were already old by the fourteenth century. The larger places like Paris, Orleans, Rouen, Lyons, Toulouse and Metz had been urban centers in Roman times. Newly chartered towns were founded and peopled during the thirteenth century. The furniture of this time was sparse, consisting of crude tables, chairs, chests, and cupboards. Babies had cradles set on rockers. The rocking chair had not yet been invented by the American, Benjamin Franklin.

Bourgeois ladies often used polished brass plaques to see themselves in.

By the fourteenth century, bourgeois families had bathrooms with wooden tubs in their houses. A bath accessory was an elegant shift of linen or cotton which shielded the bather's nudity from the servants.

Francis I (1515–1547) was sometimes a crony of Henry VIII of England. They had much in common, enjoying hunting, women, magnificence of dress, and love of life in general.

Henry II (1547–1559) was romantically attached to Diane de

Poitiers for twenty-three years. At his death, his wife, Catherine de Medici, sent her packing posthaste.

Henry IV (1589–1610), often criticized during his lifetime, was universally mourned at his death. Shortly before being assassinated he said "They will see what I was worth when I am gone." His prophecy came true.

Women of the Louis XIII (1610–1643) period received admirers while resting in or on their beds, dressed in fine robes and with fur coverlets on their feet.

The first shop selling objets d'art brought from the Far East opened in Paris in 1610.

During the first part of the reign of Louis XIII the process of veneering appeared.

Engravings and paintings show us examples of early French furniture. A sixteenth-century miniature of a lady in the court of Queen Anne of Brittany is shown weeping for an absent husband during the Italian War, seated at a trestle table on a straight-back bench.

In the sixteenth century, furniture was still scarce, but textiles were used lavishly, tossed over chairs, benches, stools, hung over and around beds, and on walls.

Henry III (1560–1574) occasionally appeared at official ceremonies dressed as a woman, and was nicknamed "the King of Sodom." Nevertheless, he had several affairs with women and was considered an excellent husband.

Louis XIII (1610–1643) did not consummate his marriage to Anne of Austria for four years. They had their first child after twenty years of marriage.

Until the time of Louis XIV (1643–1715), not even the king had each of his homes (palaces) furnished. The furniture was moved from place to place as the monarch moved.

From medieval times infant princes had two cradles (des berceaux). They had a plain one for everyday use and a richly decorated cradle with costly coverings for display. Some were made of gold or silver.

By the sixteenth century, the chair was a common piece of furniture.

Louis XIV, known as "The Sun King" (Le Roi Soleil), came to the throne in 1643 at the age of ten. He chose the sun as his emblem because he believed the earth drew its sustenance from the sun, and the life of France from his person.

Louis XV's consort, Marie Leczinska, disliked cold weather so intensely that she spent a fortune on coverlets for her bed. One would think that it was warmer in France than in Poland where she came from. She was twenty-three years old and he was fifteen years old when they married. Obviously, he did not keep her warm.

The cabriole leg originated in China in the Tang dynasty. In France the cabriole leg terminated in hoof, scroll or tapered feet. In England and America they usually terminated in Dutch pad, claw, or claw-and-ball feet.

When Jeanne Antoinette Poisson, the future Madame de Pompadour, was nine years old, she was told by a fortune-teller that she would become the mistress of the king. From that moment she began to prepare for that role. Even her family began to call her "Reinette," the little queen. That's job preparation!

It is true that Marie Antoinette liked beautiful things, but it was Madame de Pompadour who had greater perception concerning the visual arts, coupled with knowledge and appreciation.

In the novel "Robinson Crusoe" by Daniel Defoe (1719), Robinson Crusoe and Friday traveled through the provinces of Languedoc, Gascony and Toulouse, then to Paris, and on to Dover after they were rescued from the remote island in the Brazils. On the Gascony side of the mountain, Friday killed a bear.

The Louis XIV period (1774–1793) favored suites of furniture and sets of chairs.

It was the custom in various regions to plant a tree at the birth of a child. The tree was cut down to celebrate his or her grandchild's birth and to make an armoire for that child.

In many parts of France, the showpiece of the household was the armoire. It was part of the bride's dowry, and ordered soon after she was born. But the metal mounts, hinges, locks, and lock plates were not added until after her engagement was announced. By custom they were to be provided by the prospective bridegroom's parents.

Fine city mansions, owned by bishops, lords, knights, and royal officers were called hôtels.

The dining room made its appearance about 1680 and the salon drawing room in the eighteenth century.

During the seventeenth century, the salon became the principal room where the aristocratic or middle-class woman spent much of her time.

The sunflower, usually considered a uniquely American detail, is found on Louis XVI cabinets. Designs travelled both ways across the ocean.

Many fine pieces of French furniture were sold to English collectors by French aristocrats fleeing the terror of the French Revolution.

Carved or painted five-pointed stars were thought to ward away evil.

The six-pointed star of David was considered the lucky star of the brewers.

In the eighteenth century, study walls were sometimes hung with leather from Cordova.

Louis XVI console tables are similar to those of English Robert Adam console tables circa 1780.

The coronation wardrobe of Napoleon, Josephine, and Napoleon's court was designed by the theatrical designer, Jean-Baptiste Isabey.

Napoleon decreed that armchairs were to be reserved for the Empress Josephine and his mother, Letizia Bonaparte. All other members of the court were ordered to sit on stools. This is apparent in period paintings of the Court.

When Louis XVIII came to power he lived with Napoleon's used furniture. There was no money for new pieces, but the bees were removed and fleur de lys and L's were substituted.

George Washington bought French furnishings. Thomas Jefferson learned about French culture and furniture while minister to France. John Quincy Adams also purchased some French furniture. James Monroe ordered French furniture for the White House while president.

Between ten and twenty-five thousand French immigrants arrived in America after the French Revolution of 1789 and settled principally in New York City, Albany, and Baltimore, Maryland. Many brought their French furniture with them to America.

Queen Victoria bought a table for Prince Albert, for the

Christmas of 1855, from the Paris Exhibition in the Louis XVI style. It had beautiful marquetry with porcelain plaques, and mounts of gilt bronze and silvered metal. The marquetry depicted love birds. The marriage coffer of Marie Antoinette with a center design of love birds on a quiver with an Oriental scene in the background was probably the inspiration for this later piece.

The American Empire period was from 1820 to 1840. Their French-influenced designs came directly from France and also via England.

General Charles de Gaulle preferred Empire furniture.

FROM MEDIEVAL GOTHIC TO THE ITALIAN RENAISSANCE INFLUENCE AND FRANCIS I

Medieval French furniture was designed for a feudal, unstable, and constantly warring society. The furniture was constructed of oak, simply made, sturdy, usually unadorned, and most important, transportable. These early pieces were designed to be disassembled when moving, and reassembled on arrival. Hence the word "mobilier" (moveable property). Impressive coffers (chests) survive from the years 1400 to 1500, some in native Gothic styles and others in the imported Italian Renaissance styles. In the Middle Ages, French carvers established their well-deserved reputation.

In the eleventh century, Romanesque builders experimented with a pointed arch (a thrust and counterthrust) that eventually replaced the earlier curved Roman arch. While all medieval pointed architecture has been classed as Gothic, the most complete embodiment was seen in France. It was complemented by Gothic church furniture, Gothic court pieces, and crude household necessities in the Gothic style such as chests. As in England, many of the finest French craftsmen worked primarily for the church.

Most furniture from the Middle Ages has disappeared due to its original scarcity, fires, floods, furniture insects, and constant transport, and the fact that wood is easily damaged.

The coffer (chest) was usually the first piece of furniture ordered. It provided storage, seating, sleeping, and dining functions. Extant chests from the fourteenth century are hard to recognize because of extensive repairs. Museums own various early coffers constructed of crude planks held together with iron bands. The chest changed after the fourteenth century. It no longer needed iron bands to hold it together, but could be made strong with complex joints such as the dovetail. In the fifteenth and sixteenth centuries the chestmakers went a step further. They began to construct carved panelled chests. These early Gothic chests consisted of thick uprights and traverses with mortice-and-tenon joints. The pointed Gothic arch, which appeared in these chests, may have been introduced into France by the Normans, who had seen them in Sicily. Many early pieces were enriched with paint. These early French pieces often combined Gothic and Romanesque designs and later combined Gothic with Italian Renaissance designs.

For decoration, chestmakers used arches filled with undulating curves, enclosing rosettes, quatrefoils or linenfold carving. The metalwork on the chest became part of the decoration. The locks consisted of a metal box, attractively designed, containing the bolt, and attached with visible nails. Some chests had iron work borders cut out to resemble lace. The hasp, which was hinged on to a piece of iron work decoration was itself decorated with beetles, salamanders, chimeras, dragons, and human busts.

As early as 1254 the Provost of Paris ordained that chestmakers should have their own guild.

In the early thirteenth century, the furniture of castles had primitive simplicity. In the great hall there was a long massive oak table with benches and stools. At the end of the table there was a large armchair, overhung with a canopy of silk. The walls were decorated with tapestry, and the floor was paved with hard stone or tile. The bedroom had a bed with or without curtains and a box or chest for clothes and seating. Perhaps a prie-dieu chair was present.

The bench was seen early in the thirteenth century. It was also called a form or forme. This, too, was an adaptation of the chest, now with a back and arm rests. There was a small bench for one person called a benchlet, banchel, bancel or a stool (escabeau).

The late fourteenth and the fifteenth century was a period of transition. Many nobles who owned fortified castles in the country now began to build houses in towns and cities as well. A great change took place in castles in the late fourteenth and fifteenth centuries. Textile materials transformed interiors. Textile furnishings had the advantage of being folded or rolled for packing. Carpets were laid on the hard floors, cushions of gold cloth were important additions, and fine chairs of leather embellished with stamped designs and silk fringe and studded with nails replaced plainer chairs. Walls were hung with embroidered satin tapestries, and vases were made of fine silver. Beds were large and hung with rich materials. A new social life was beginning and these new houses needed domestic furniture.

The throne chair (chaire; also called chaiere) was a

fifteenth-century piece that paralleled the English great chair. It is actually a chest with the rear uprights extended to form a high back, and the side uprights extended to form arm rests. The base is the chest which usually was fitted with a lock. The back is the only decorated part but does not start below the point level with the owner's head. The reverse side of the chair was never decorated. English great chairs were often more highly decorated with the entire back and arms carved.

The buffet or dressoir (dresser) was also derived from the chest. These are chests mounted on feet that open at the front. There was the buffet de parade that was used for displaying gold and silver plates for special ceremonies. The simple buffet was made in various ways. The simplest was a rectangular box with two compartments called guichets that were closed in with doors called vantaux. The doors are placed on either side of a central upright, a panel, or a blind panel. On this piece of furniture, we see for the first time frieze drawers or layettes. Some buffets just have small rectangular panels below the large ones. The base is left open; a single panel at the back is joined to the two, three or four front uprights by arched or flattened stretchers bracketed together. The ornamentation is copied from the fifteenth-century chest and is regulated by the division of the panels. However, geometric and floral motifs began to appear as a result of the Renaissance. As with the chests, richly designed locks add to the decoration of the buffets.

Prior to the beginning of the sixteenth century, the Italian Renaissance was carried by Francis I, the Dukes of Burgundy, and other important families to France. They viewed the new art forms during a military expedition to Italy in the spring of 1495. The French became fascinated with the Italian artistic achievements. This fascination was the beginning of the ultimate French furniture achievement.

During the reign of Francis I (1515–1547) Italian Renaissance ornaments appeared on existing French Gothic pieces. Francis invited Leonardo da Vinci to France, who arrived bringing with him previously painted masterpieces such as the "Mona Lisa," and subsequently executed commissions for his new patron. Francis supported all the arts and held a brilliant court in Paris. His palace at Fontainebleau combined French and Italian craftsmanship and designs which are known as the Francis I style or the First Renaissance.

Renaissance furniture designs favored walnut over previously preferred oak. Walnut proved to be a better wood for carving Renaissance designs, having a finer grain, more natural oil, and also a rich dark tone. Now the carvers could execute elaborate forms of decoration such as composite capitals, heads, palmettos, acanthus leaves, caryatids, strap work, bosses, masks, and arabesques.

Most French furniture in the sixteenth century, however, retained simplicity, solid construction, and was massive and rectilinear in shape. The pieces were usually chairs, stools, hutches, cupboards, and, of course, the chest. New pieces were not in common use. What might be found in an important sixteenth-century French house? Perhaps a medieval family coffer, the new dresser with the upper section raised on column supports enclosed by two or more doors, an armoire with one large door, possibly an upholstered chair, a table with elaborate supports and stretchers, heavy structural chairs, a daybed (lit de repos), a backless bench, or a gossiping chair (chaise caquetoire), and a low stool covered with tapestry called a placet.

The sixteenth-century caquetoire chair suited women wearing a farthingale (a hoop). The English made a similar chair for the same purpose but the area above the back of the seat was open and the seat was lower, while the French chair had a solid back that was flush with the seat, was higher, and was vertically stretchered. This chair evokes a strangely Oriental image.

By the late sixteenth century, the chair had become a common piece of furniture.

HENRY II, HENRY IV, AND LOUIS XIII
(1547–1643)—THE RENAISSANCE CONTINUES

Under Henry II (1547–1599) and his Florentine wife, Catherine de Medici, French cabinetmakers applied Renaissance architecture to furniture design. The artisans were often sculptors, architects, and designers. Pattern books of ornamental furnishings began to be closely followed. The Henry II style had originality, and a classic quality was seen emerging. By the close of the sixteenth century French Gothic dominance ended, and the Italian Renaissance was the major influence on French furniture. Henry II style was called "High Renaissance." Francis I style had been called "First Renaissance."

In 1608 Henry IV (1589–1610) established royal workshops in the Louvre galleries to encourage French craftsmanship. Luxury court pieces were, at this time, imported from Italy, Spain, and Germany. Henry dreamed of the finest furniture being French, and made by French artists. The craftsmen who worked at the Louvre, however, were mostly foreigners or French artists that Henry had sent to Flanders to study. Now furniture was being made in France for the court. French national furniture, as an art form, had not fully developed, although the French character was evolving. Ultimately, the ambition of Henry IV was achieved, but it happened fifty years later under Louis XIV.

Henry's second wife, Marie de Medici, although born in Florence, Italy, was partial to Flemish art. It was she, acting as regent, who brought Jean Macé from the Netherlands about 1620. His expertise in veneering helped to revolutionize French furniture.

Henry IV not only desired fine furniture for members of the aristocracy, but also for the French public that could afford it. This consideration was unusual for a French king. Henry was also responsible for the establishment of the tapestry industry known as "Savonnerie," the silk industry at Lyons and Tours, and the manufacture of porcelain.

The Louis XIII period (1610–1643) that followed Henry IV

failed to achieve a singular French product because French design was still being influenced by craftsmen from the Netherlands, Spain, and Holland. Art forms from the Far East also affected the furniture scene. Chinese and Japanese influences had been fashionable since Portugal created the General Company of the Indies. Oriental textiles also played an important design role at this time.

The most important furniture piece during this period was the cabinet. The great cabinetmakers working at this time were Pierre Boulee and Coffieri. Veneering that had begun under Henry IV continued and was the highlight of fine cabinetry. Later the development of varnishing on ebony produced exceptional pieces.

The bed became a conspicuous piece of furniture with a heavily-decorated canopy, adorned with silks, silver or gold ornaments, and even ostrich feathers. Society ladies received admirers while they reclined on these beds, wearing luxurious robes and covering their feet with furs.

There was, however, some modification of furniture in the Louis XIII period. Decorations and forms grew heavier and coarser. Plumes and crossed plumes occurred more often. Cartouches grew bigger and their edges were thicker. Panels were cut in a variety of geometric combinations: lozenges enclosing squares, lozenges divided into triangles, and diamond-point decoration where the surface was studded with little pyramids. Furniture had inlay of stones, metals, tortoise-shell, ivory, and bone. But the truly golden age of French decoration was about to dawn with the Sun King.

LOUIS XIV (1643–1715)—A SINGULAR FRENCH STYLE EMERGES

During the reign of Louis XIV a singular, genuinely French style began to surface. For two centuries France had turned to other countries for furniture style, but now a new wave of artistic development came into being. Louis XIV deserves the credit for engineering this artistic success by putting many elements into play simultaneously.

Now architecture influenced interior design. A grand plan for incorporating external and internal spaces, including walls, ceilings, floors, furniture, and all decorative elements resulted in artistic compatibility between furniture and space. No longer would newly designed furniture be placed in rooms regardless of their interior architecture. This set the pattern for the future, most recently in the 1930s when modern architecture and modern furniture made a bold design statement.

Louis XIV had a dream of creating glorious palaces and impressing the whole world. It took many great artists and craftsmen to fulfill his ambition. It also took tremendous coordination. And yes, the world was very impressed.

Jean Baptiste Colbert (1619–1693) the superintendent of royal palaces, ordered the erection of new buildings and brought together the finest artists and craftsmen to furnish and decorate them. The artist, Charles Lebrun, was put in charge. He administered and coordinated the work of architects, sculptors, painters, weavers, goldsmiths, cabinetmakers, and engravers. The monumental task of furnishing the Louvre, Versailles, the Trianon, Fontainebleau, Saint Germain, and Marly began. The king did not blink even when artisans made special furniture out of solid silver. Cost was not a consideration.

The menuisier and the ébéniste (carver and cabinetmaker) were now required to follow the designs of the maitres ornemanistes who had a comprehensive plan laid out for the total development of the palace. Foreign influences were no longer paramount.

During this period the art of veneering was a common practice. Marquetry was also an important element in furniture decoration. André Charles Boulle's marquetry was so wonderful that pieces decorated with the style of marquetry he produced are called "Boulle" furniture. Boulle also used secondary materials such as brass, pewter, and tortoise-shell. This master is famous for his finely designed bronze mounts that were chased and gilded. These were affixed on the most exposed parts of furniture, originally to protect their edges and vulnerable areas. Bas-reliefs, medallions, friezes and masks were used to hold marquetry from slipping. Keyhole plates or handles were anchored with large mounts that protected vulnerable spots from key scratches or fingernail gouges. Pendants, corners and cornices, as well as legs, were also protected by bronze mounts. Many tried, but no one ever copied Boulle pieces with the success achieved by this master.

A sharp distinction was drawn between the cabinetmakers who worked in solid wood called "menuisiers en bois," and those who worked with veneers and marquetry, called "menuisiers an ébène."

Wood gilding was known since the fourteenth century, but now it was generally applied to furniture. Richly carved chairs, canapés, and tables in the royal suites were often totally gilded.

Lacquer was new to French furniture making and was the result of the French fascination with Chinese and Japanese furniture, Oriental porcelain, and fabrics. Furniture which was varnished similarly to Oriental pieces was called "Chinese style." The Louis XIV period marks the introduction of this technique into the impressive French furniture picture.

Symmetry was important in the furniture design of the Louis XIV period. Furniture lines continue straight but are more relaxed than those in the Louis III period. Garlands of flowers and tassels softened the hard straight lines of chairs and armoires. Curves are adopted, but have not the graceful lines that will emerge under Louis XV. Tables were designed in many shapes such as round, square, and pentagonal. They were made of wood with gilt, marble, porphyry, and ebony. Many of these tables were lavishly decorated. The friezes were enriched with profuse carving. Legs were in baluster form, designed with caryatids, or with S-shaped legs, and cross-stretchered on extremely heavy pieces. When the console table was adopted, the legs were simplified and the back legs disappeared as the wall served for the support.

The Louis XIV armchair has a high back, is completely covered in upholstery, has wooden arm rests that are curved and scrolled, has a square seat that is supported by carved or moulded legs, and has H-shaped stretchers.

A richly carved tapering pillar leg with a bold capital was also used during this period. Toward the end of the century the famous cabriole leg was introduced, and terminated in the pied de boche or cloven hoof foot. Chairs with flat stretchers in an X formation often had a decorative centerpiece. Upholstery on Louis XIV chairs was usually fastened with large gilt or silvered nail heads. Long fringe was another form of decoration.

About the middle of the seventeenth century, the canapé, a type of small sofa, appeared. They were often made en suite with tall upholstered armchairs. The earliest ones had upholstered wings called joues. Various canapés resemble two or three assembled armchairs that do not have wings.

Beds in this period were monumental and were heavily decorated with exotic and expensive fabrics.

An ornately decorated oblong ebony cabinet mounted on a gilded stand with an elaborate interior was typical of the Louis XIV period. Decorations included marquetry of wood, metal, stone mosaic work, tortoise shell, and bronze mounts.

Panelling is found on walnut and oak cupboards. Moldings are strong and heavy, especially on cornices.

The dining room was a new room, emerging in the 1680s.

A very important aspect of this time are the simpler pieces produced for the middle class, such as armchairs, stools, armoires, and tables. In the chapter on "Regional Furniture," these pieces are discussed in detail. It should be noted that production of Louis XIV furniture was not limited to Paris, but was made throughout France in many regional styles.

RÉGENCE (1700–1723)

The style known as Régence was a narrow transitional period between the styles of Louis XIV and Louis XV. It is named for Philippe d'Orleans, the nephew of Louis XIV, who was appointed regent for Louis XV. Louis XV was five years old when his great-grandfather died.

The Régence period includes the time between 1700 and 1723. The furniture is architectural and symmetrical. Régence elements are modified Louis XIV designs and emerging Louis XV elements. These pieces incorporated both influences but managed to retain a lovely form. They preclude the asymmetry of rococo styles. The furniture pieces are solid and heavy, but the twining vines and twigs that branch out from their uprights break up the severe structural forms. Corners of square frames were often decorated with shells and flowers. The old shell shape is now jagged or pierced and even the leaf carvings are lighter. The cabriole legs which had been introduced late in the Louis XIV period were fashionable.

Private houses were designed to be more intimate and therefore furniture became smaller to complement the new dimensions. The invention of mirror-glass cast in sheets gave spaciousness to the fashionable smaller rooms. The dining room arrived in the 1680s and the salon drawing room would emerge in the eighteenth century. Marquetry was colorful but not as admired as veneers of rosewood and other woods having a violet or purple hue.

The cabinetmaker to Philippe d'Orleans was Charles Cressent. His chest of drawers with a "crossbow" silhouette was known as "profile en arbalète." Régence pieces often had bronze decorations, some with exotic Chinese or Turkish motifs. Cressent designed a singular mount in the shape of a feminine Spanish head that was called an espagnolle.

Régence commodes were massive and heavy, with cabriole legs, and swelled sides. They were made with wood veneers and bronze accessories.

Armoires were lovely with veneers, cross-banding, and slightly bowed doors.

Writing tables were important pieces, many of which were made in Liège.

In these years caned chairs became very popular. They were similar to the Louis XIV chairs but more rounded, with lower seats and padded armrests.

This was the period when local craftsmen, working with local woods, began to create regional pieces that simplified the important court styles. We refer to much of this furniture as "country French," "rustic," or "provincial." It is discussed by province in a separate chapter.

Next comes the flowering of French furniture, under Louis XV, when masterpieces of unrivaled elegance will be created.

Louis XV (1715–1774)

Louis XV furniture is perhaps the finest furniture ever made! It is simply exquisite and made with dazzling virtuosity. Fortunately, many masterpieces from this period survived "The Terror," permitting the world to enjoy these remarkable pieces.

During the reign of Louis XV the French cabinetmakers or ébénistes were the most talented in Europe. They were freed from the "grand designs" of previous periods and were allowed to execute furniture with individuality and singular imagination. The Royal Courts of foreign countries now ordered French furniture or tried to copy it. The dream of Henry IV had materialized.

Louis XV married the Polish princess, Marie Leczinska, who was dull, dowdy, and pious. She was so pious that she denied Louis her bed on the feast days of all the major saints, and, as she grew older, her list of major saints grew much longer.

His mistress, Madame de Pompadour, was a complete contrast. She was a fine amateur actress, sang sweetly, danced divinely, drew, played the clavichord, dressed with great elegance, kept a delicious table, entertained with flair, and had a beautiful figure. She was also a very loving person.

Madame de Pompadour's other passions were building, decorating, and redecorating houses. She was a great collector and amassed valuable and unique objects. She promoted a new simplicity in many of her residences. She was very fond of imitation lacquer pieces. After 1745 she encouraged the rococo style.

At this time both the Court and the wealthy Parisians spent fantastic amounts of money on their interior decorations. They wanted new and wonderful pieces and rejected anything that was dated. Dealers and craftsmen were more than happy to fulfill their desires. Unhappily, supplying the aristocrats and court did not guarantee prompt payments.

It was fashionable to change upholstery with the seasons.

In the winter, velvet and damask fabrics were used, and silk and cotton fabrics were used for the spring and summer months.

The major characteristic of the Louis XV period is Rocaille work known as Rococo. It is absolutely charming and it combined fantastic shapes with true-to-life images. There is no regard for symmetry with monkeys, bows, ribbons, dogs, shells, and flying birds, flowers, and trelliswork swirled together with taste and balance on chairs and cabinet pieces.

Nicolas Pineau was a great rococo furniture designer during this period. These highly curved pieces are not determined by architecture, but for the desires of a voluptuous society dedicated to pleasure. Interestingly, Louis XV salons were not crowded with furniture, seldom having more than ten pieces at the most.

The decorative elements associated with Louis XV furniture include veneer, marquetry in geometric and floral designs, cube parquetry, bronze mounts, mosaic work, lacquer work, varnishing and carving. Carved giltwood console tables and mirrors stayed in fashion. Floral carvings, especially roses, were a favorite motif. Porcelain plaques for enrichment of various pieces reached a peak around 1766. Many varieties of marble were used on commodes and table tops.

A new piece was the "chiffonnier," a tall chest consisting of a number of drawers.

At first, tables retained the heavy Louis XIV shape with the exception of the console table. Cross-stretchers were used less frequently. Cabriole legs with a double bend that had an S or scroll shape with feet called "pied-de-biche" (hoofed foot) are an important element on tables.

The seating pieces were of various designs. Those with a flat back were called "sièges à la Reine," and those with a concave back "sièges en cabriole." The typical Louis XV chair has a lower back than a Louis XIV or a Regency armchair. The back was not meant to be higher than the sitter's shoulders. Also, the seat is lower. The legs are cabriole in shape and cross-stretchers were not needed for these lighter chairs.

The "bergère" is an armchair with a loose seat cushion and upholstered arms.

The "marquise" might be called a tête-à-tête, and can seat two people. It is a wider and deeper piece than the bergère.

The "fauteuil en confessional," which was also called a wing chair in earlier periods, has a high back and solid sides that end in small projections called wings or joues.

The "fauteuil de cabinet" is a desk chair with a semicircular curve to the rear of the seat and a pronounced curve in the front of the seat. One leg supports the front seat rail, another at the center of the back, and the other two support the scrolled arm rests. Some were made with five legs, and they were often caned or upholstered in leather.

The "fauteuil à coiffer" was a dressing table chair, often caned.

The "voyeuse" was like the armchair, with a flat, curved toprail on which one could place one's elbows, perhaps while watching a card game.

The "canapé" was a settee, and a sopha (sofa) was a canapé with a lower seat and was completely upholstered (about five inches long).

The "Duchesse" was a chaise lounge, but when it was extended by stools, it was called "brisé." The "veilleuse" was a daybed with a third back.

The "lit de repos" or "lit du jour" was a daybed, and may have one or two raised sides.

The "ottomane" (ottoman) is a small canapé with an oval seat: The back follows the contours of the seat and is lower at the front. The "turquoise" is similar to the ottomane, but its back is divided into three sections. A "paphose" is another type of ottoman but has a kidney shape and does not have armrests.

There were two major styles of beds: the French bed with one headboard, and the Polish bed with a canopy that was hung from the ceiling or attached to the wall. The Polish bed might have two or three raised sides.

Writing tables, important in the Régence period, continue to be important.

Gaming tables were designed for the particular game that was to be played on them.

There were bureau plats with three drawers, with the middle drawer slightly recessed.

Commodes that were massive in the Régence period were now scaled down.

Due to the discoveries at Pompeii and Herculaneum, enthusiasm for the rococo waned. The French always wanted new motifs. Now neoclassic taste will emerge, although transitional pieces will retain the curved lines of rococo with ornaments in the new style. This is the end of an exquisite era, the likes of which were never seen again.

LOUIS XVI STYLE (1774–1793)

This style actually began during the reign of Louis XV, about 1765. It is common for styles to overlap and most periods have transitional pieces. This period turned away from the twenty rococo years and found its inspiration in antiquity. The discovery of Herculaneum and Pompeii brought renewed interest in ancient Rome, and designers were quick to interpret these ancient motifs. Thus, the Louis XVI style is an adaptation of antiquity to French furniture craftsmanship. As in the past, the French constantly delighted in new furniture styles.

This furniture was made of mahogany without decoration, or with new details such as strips of bronze covered with parallel ridges, women's busts adopted from Egyptian art, winged sphinxes and silhouettes of draped women balancing baskets on their heads. Ornaments such as Greek-key borders, rosettes, laurel-wreaths, palmettes, acanthus leaves, pearls, ovolos, gadroons, knot-work, twisting ribbons and quivers inspired by past classical designs reappear. Designs like quivers and Egyptian figures will be very important on coming Empire pieces. Another new detail of the period was the use of lattice-work balustrades.

Most furniture of the Louis XVI period had the same shape as pieces from the previous period of Louis XV. One new piece was the "fauteuil à chapeau," a hat-like easy chair with a slightly arched back.

Mahogany furniture was new, and mahogany chairs had latticework backs decorated with lyres, sheaves of corn and baskets. French commodes of the Louis XVI period were rectangular, semicircular or straight, with only simple rods (strips) of brass. The "bonheur-de-jour" (happiness of the day) was a table topped with a small cabinet with a niche which sometimes contained dummy books. Metal furniture, such as work tables, pedestal tables, and luncheon tables were popular and were made of wrought iron and steel.

The Louis XVI period had many outstanding cabinet-makers. Three important ones were Jean Henri Riesener, George Jacob and M. Carlin. Riesener was Ébéniste du Roi from 1774 to 1784. The most characteristic features of Carlin's work were his use of lacquer, the quality of his mounts, pietro-dure decorations, and the feminine and graceful contours of his pieces. George Jacob was first known for his chairs and beds, but later for all kinds of pieces and suites. His most important commission was for a suite he made for Queen Marie Antoinette. Jean Henri Riesener excelled in majestic pieces and collaborated with the carver, Gouthiére, inventor of the gilding known as "au mat," which enhanced the beauty of bronze fittings. Riesener is also famous for the "bureau à cylindre" (roll or cylinder top desk). The prototype was begun by Oeben and completed by Riesener in 1769. He was most famous for his exquisite marquetry.

This period saw veneered and marquetry pieces of exquisite design. The use of mahogany was becoming more important during this time. Mahogany was used solid for seat pieces as well as for its veneers. Satinwood and ebony were also becoming fashionable again. Floral marquetry in colorful woods was still favored by cabinetmakers such as Riesener. Plaques of porcelain were inserted into furniture, and varnishes and lacquers continued to please.

Solid wood armoires were rare and were usually the work of provincial workshops and kept to Louis XV designs. These are pieces collectors often look for. The glass cabinet called the "vitrine," which is a small cupboard with glass panes instead of solid doors, is a Louis XVI piece. The bookcase or "bibliothèque" was another rather new piece. It was usually made in two sections with the lower part closed and the upper part with glass panes or wire trelliswork. At this juncture the dining table, influenced by the English dining table, began to gain favor. The "jardinière" was a rectangular box on legs for flowers and was called a "table à fleurs."

DIRECTOIRE (REVOLUTIONARY)

This style extends over three political regimes: the Revolutionary government (1789–1795), the Directory (1795–1799), and the Consulate (1799–1804). At this time transitional designs merge and overlap previous styles. In 1789, furniture was still being made in the Louis XVI style, but by 1804, French furniture turned to the Empire style.

Several trends are found during this period. Some of the ébénistes of the old regime stayed with the old styles. Some simply stopped working before the Directors even assumed power. Others adjusted immediately and adapted themselves to whatever new style was demanded. A few of the young cabinetmakers who had been well trained looked forward to emerging styles and to establishing themselves. Painters and architects had a direct effect on the styles of the period.

Beginnings of the Directoire style were seen in the latter years of Louis XVI's reign. The famous artist Jacques Louis David ordered Etruscan furniture for his studio at the Louvre in 1789 and used some of these pieces in his paintings. In 1790 the designer, Jean-Demosthené Dugourc, produced furniture models with Etruscan elements intermingled with Greek motifs.

Orators of the French Revolution praised the moral values of antiquity and endorsed a style which evoked an ancient and glorious past.

Sadly, tremendous quantities of irreplaceable furniture were burned beneath a "Tree of Liberty," and great national treasures perished at this terrible time.

At this juncture the guilds were abolished, official identification stamps were suppressed, and veneering and marquetry were seldom used. Inlay work, however, was used, made from ebony, satinwood, brass, and pewter.

Directoire furniture was constructed with solid woods, often beech. A great amount was painted in light colors such as blue or green with gold enrichment. Mahogany veneers or solid carved mahogany were only for a few luxury pieces. Furniture shapes became simpler and mounts were also simplified, often made of brass rather than traditional gilt-bronze. This furniture is an austere imitation of classical art.

Decoration of Directoire furniture was often inspired by military motifs, such as spears, helmets, crossed swords, pikes, and lances. The palmetto is also seen on bands, friezes, and as an applied ornament. Egyptian designs of sphinxes, scarabs, caryatids, and pyramids were popular. Lozenge designs were painted or inlaid to frame central motifs. Many geometrical shapes are found on this furniture. Realistic and fanciful animals were also used on Directoire pieces. Revolutionary emblems were popular at this time, including scenes such as "Storming of the Bastille" and "Trees of Liberty."

After 1799 Napoleon ended the further destruction of French treasures. He personally supervised the rebuilding of furniture manufacturing with renewed standards. He desired new furniture fit for an emperor.

During this period, "Directory" and "Empire" style furniture was made only in Paris, while the rest of the country continued to produce Louis XIV- and Louis XV-style furniture.

EMPIRE

Empire style is named for the period of the First Empire (1804–1815). Empire furniture has been called cold and has not always been appreciated or even desired. Much of it was obviously concerned with looking imperial.

Empire style was a continuation of the styles from the last years of the monarchy. Late Louis XVI furniture had become austere. It was greatly influenced by the excavations at Herculaneum and Pompeii. Although the French Revolution of 1789 changed the destiny of France, it did not greatly affect the arts, including furniture design.

What does Empire furniture look like? Whereas Directoire pieces were often painted in light colors, Empire furniture tended to be in dark wood or gilt. The use of moldings was almost abandoned, and when used, narrowed down to a fillet or a flat narrow band. Smooth, round columns with bronze bases and capitals are an important element of Empire pieces. This furniture has sharp corners and looks angular and severe. The cabinetwork is block-like and has large surfaces of polished mahogany and heavy bases. Empire furniture is symmetrical, as are the motifs used on it. Mahogany was the most frequently used wood during this period, either in veneer or in solid form. Knot elm was popular due to its reddish color that was similar to mahogany. Maple and lemon woods were used for light-colored bedroom suites. Walnut and beech, long favorites, were now avoided. Marquetry and lacquer work were also out of favor at this time. The inlaying of bands of contrasting woods such as ebony with mahogany was a decorative detail.

Decorating furniture surfaces with gilded bronze mounts or appliques was the most important feature of this period. Although gilded bronze mounts had been seen since the Louis XIV period, never were they used more than in this period. These bronze mounts were generally flat and complemented the dark mahogany surfaces they appeared on.

The cabinetmakers frequently omitted handles on drawers, and it was necessary to pull out the drawers by means of a key placed in the keyhole, which was unobtrusive. When handles were used, they were in the form of either a round or flat small knob ornamented with rosettes or loose-ring handles attached to a circular back plate at the top.

The delights of this furniture were the wonderful supports for chairs and tables, made of bronze, wood, or a combination of these elements. The designs of these supports consisted of winged sphinxes, winged lions, chimeras with eagle's heads, and lion monopodium composed of the head and chest of a lion that concluded with the paw. Another motif was an elongated bust of a woman mounted on a pillar that rested on two human feet often made of gilt bronze. American Empire pieces from Maryland also used this motif. Swans were also a decorative motif, frequently found as arm posts for chairs and sofas as well as composing entire arms.

The most familiar motifs of the period were: acanthus leaves woven into a wreath, Greek palm leaves, rosettes, stars, swags, arabesques, medallions, winged classical figures, Olympian gods and goddesses, allegorical subjects, emblems of victory, and imperial emblems such as the eagle. Egyptian motifs such as lotus capitals, sphinxes, winged globes, vases, Roman chariots, winged trumpets, cornucopias, Neptunes, tridents, amphora, flowers, garlands, bay leaves, laurel boughs, and vines were also used, all characterized by their formal stiff depiction.

The bees and the wreaths are the most familiar designs to appear on Empire pieces during the Napoleonic period. The "bees" were designed to replace the "fleur de lys" of the old monarchy.

THE RESTORATION

This is the period between 1815 to 1850. It is called the "Restoration" because the monarchy was restored to power. Louis XVIII ruled from 1814 to 1824.

When Louis came to power he lived with Napoleon's old furniture. There were simply no funds available for new pieces. Napoleon's bees were removed, and fleur de lys and L's were substituted.

The aristocracy who survived the revolution had very few remaining possessions. They were glad to be alive and would happily use Napoleon's "hand-me-downs." When they were finally able to afford new pieces the aristocracy looked to the cabinetmakers who had furnished their homes in the past.

New pieces combined old and new designs. Bronze mounts were no longer considered a necessity. Straight lines softened.

Charles X was king from 1824 to 1830. He favored neo-Gothic, neo-Egyptian, and Oriental designs.

During the late 1820s and 1830s imitation Oriental lacquer (japanning) was popular, often found on Louis XVI revival style pieces. The use of Chinese and Japanese lacquer panels was a revival of Louis XV and Louis XVI materials.

Louis-Philippe I came to the throne in 1830 and stayed until 1848. His influence showed in heavy pieces, dark woods, broad cornices, and industrial machine-made furniture.

The 1850s saw a revival of Renaissance-style furniture. The French colony of Vietnam was the source of many Oriental-style fantasy pieces.

There were three concurrent Louis revivals. The first was Louis XVI from 1815 to 1840. Next came Louis XV from 1830 to 1930. The third revival was Louis XVI again from 1850 to 1900.

The aristocracy was composed of a small group with little ready money. Most new furniture was ordered by the emerging middle class. They lived in apartments, not mansions, and needed pieces suitable for family life. These people did not have the knowledge of furniture that the former ruling class took for granted. They settled for smaller pieces, native woods, and generally less ornate designs. These pieces, while simpler, were not austere. The austerity and grandeur of Napoleon were not required and would have looked out of place in their smaller apartments.

Furniture made during the Restoration was constructed before the manufacture of furniture was completely converted to machine tools. The industrial revolution here, as in England, would forever change the way furniture would be made. Therefore, early Restoration pieces, while not particularly original in design, are valuable for their construction.

Moldings appeared again and carving regained popularity. Inlay work, not seen for years, also made a comeback. Veneers were constructed with most colorful woods. While mahogany was the most important wood, walnut, maple, and ash gained admirers.

Decoration became more informal. Empire-style decorations were still used but were smaller, and bronze ornaments were used less often. The lyre motif was carved, inlaid, and made as bronze mounts.

The egg-and-dart, the rosette, beading, ribbon-bands, scrollwork, marquetry, rosettes on cross-stretchers, and keyhole plates composed much of the decoration.

Chairs had padded, upholstered backs that were straight or slightly rolled over. The rear legs were saber-shaped and the front legs were often square and curved forward. Back legs splay more than they did during the Directory and Empire periods. Fantastic animal shapes often formed the arm supports.

Some chair backs had panels with trelliswork filling them. The gondola chair with its curved back and sides sloping in the seat was a favored piece.

From 1848 to 1852 industrialization continued with large, hard, contoured pieces. This time was referred to as the Second Republic.

THE SECOND EMPIRE

Napoleon III (1850–1870) furniture was essentially composed of revival pieces of the previous five hundred years. A similar recycling was taking place in England and America. As this period progressed, the effect of the Industrial Revolution was clearly evident in the amount of showy furniture mass-produced for the middle class. Machines now carved furniture and also stamped out their mounts.

Some fine handcrafted furniture was still custom ordered. Purplewood and ebony were the choice of the wealthy. Pearwood and beechwood were often stained black to imitate ebony when saving money was necessary. Neo-Renaissance pieces were constructed of oak.

The Louis XV style with added decorations was attractive to purchasers during this time. Furniture was overloaded with machine-made decorations, fringes, and tassels. It was also overloaded in England. Copies were made of Marie Antoinette's furniture but with buttoned upholstery, tassels, lace trimmings, and added fringe. It was a time of excess. America also had revival furniture but they never achieved the degree of decoration seen in France and England. This is because America never had court furniture.

Many seating pieces were completely upholstered. Bamboo and papier-mâché furniture and decorative pieces were fashionable. Table legs assumed various forms such as sphinxes, lions with open jaws and claws, chimeras, molded legs with traverses, and cabriole legs with scrolled or tapered feet.

Copies of Riesener furniture were popular, and although they did not compare with the originals, they are tempting to current collectors. This is because they are quite lovely, available, and also still affordable.

Sofas and canapés had lower seat-rails that ultimately developed into bases.

Bureaus reached eight feet in height with drawers from the top to the bottom. Some even had small shelves on their flat tops.

Dining tables stayed large. By 1825, many console tables had cornucopia forms serving as legs.

Early Napoleon III pieces are treasured as the finale of a long and prestigious furniture tradition.

REGIONAL FURNITURE

Regional furniture includes bourgeois, rustic, and well-off peasant pieces. Wonderful furniture originated outside the capital. Furniture made in the French provinces and towns are delightful and highly collectible. Featuring the styles of Louis XIII, this furniture can be traced back to the seventeenth century, but most surviving pieces are from the eighteenth and nineteenth centuries. The furniture of each area has individual characteristics that separate it from that of other provinces and towns, although all reflect major styles and periods. These pieces are influenced by styles already out of fashion in Paris. This furniture was also influenced by a region's geographic neighbors, local history, native woods, and existing financial conditions.

The style of Île-de-France and Touraine was graceful while pieces made in Burgundy were heavier and more ornamented. Furniture from Brittany was often architectural and boxy. Furniture from Lyons was somber and that of Provence rather heavy. Flanders produced highly carved cupboards influenced by the Italian Renaissance. The top element on cupboards had decorations that varied from province to province.

Almost every town had workmen capable of making furniture constructed with sound woods, carefully grooved and joined, and perhaps ornamented with carving. Provincial craftsmen often worked from furniture manuals with diagrams. These rural artists developed tasteful pieces with elegant lines, which are the hallmark of the natural ability of the French woodworker. Many collectors prize these pieces above the more elegant guild furniture made by masters. This furniture has individuality because it was usually made by a single artisan, and not collectively. In this we see a similarity between French and American craftsmen, both of whom created vigorous individual masterpieces.

Many people are surprised to learn that French townspeople were wealthy by the end of Louis XIV's reign (1715). This is not to imply that they had an abundance of furniture, but they did own four-post beds, chests, wardrobes, armoires, buffets, commodes, tables and chairs.

Furniture from the Toulouse region was first built in the 1100s. It was one of the first townships to gain a degree of freedom from the feudal system. One of the first French universities was founded in Toulouse. In the sixteenth century the Renaissance revolutionized furniture-making in this southwestern part of France. For the next two hundred years the moneyed classes, nobles, and bourgeoisie rebuilt mansions and country houses and ordered furniture to be made for them. There is nothing naive about the pieces made in Toulouse.

The cabinetmakers of Toulouse avoided oak, preferring fruitwoods, cherry, wild cherry, or walnut. Occasionally they painted their furniture gray, like their panelled walls. A piece typical of the Toulouse style would be a Louis XVI slant-top desk made of walnut with fluting decorating the front and sides. This furniture is noted for its sobriety, but is extremely well made, perhaps by Huguenots.

Lyons was the capital of Gaul and is still important as the nation's second city. Lyonnais furniture was almost always made of walnut. Casepieces were usually of imposing dimensions. Armoires were often nine feet high. The furniture had deeply-cut moldings framing luxuriant ornamentation. On these pieces you will find scrolls, acanthus leaves, griffins, and shell decorations. The Lyonnais armoire was topped with a large cornice, often with three arches. These cornices were richly decorated with shells, acanthus leaves, and griffins. Their chests were seldom straight, but have a swell-front, or a tomb shape. The tomb shape, developed in the Régence period, had three drawers and very short legs. It was accented with moldings and sometimes carved with scrolls or shells.

The name Charente applies to areas in Western France that include the old provinces of Angoumois, Aunis, and Saintonge. Its inhabitants preferred light or reddish woods like walnut, cherry, wild cherry, and pear. Usually these pieces were made of various combined woods. Elm and ash burr often appeared in panels or in inlaid ornamentation. Marquetry work was prominent and appeared on practically every piece that was valued. An unusual feature was dark highlights brushed with indelible ink to accent carvings. Their iron mounts were large and cut in finely pierced designs. Their ornamental motifs included the soup tureen, stars, Maltese crosses, vases, sawtooth borders, shells, and fans. Decorations include geometrics, diamond points, the Maltese cross, circles, flowers and marquetry. This furniture is a reserved application of Louis XV and Louis XVI styles.

Furniture identified as Dauphiné is from the province running from the Rhône River eastward to the Alps, and from Savoy in the north to Provence in the south. The capital of Dauphiné was Grenoble. People from this region made excellent furniture with fine marquetry. They used local woods such as gnarled walnut, ash burr, fruitwoods, and sycamore for veneer over a fir base. For decoration, flowers, acanthus leaves, foliated scrolls, and geometric motifs were used. They also made simpler pieces of solid walnut, devoid of decoration except for a narrow black fillet that accented its lines.

Beautifully carved and spindled panetières (bread boxes) came from this area. A vaisselier with the upper section having one side curved comes from this area. A bureau, a desk with curved flat stretchers, recalls English William and Mary pieces.

The enclosed bed, a lit mi-clos, stood on straight legs, had geometric decoration and spindles, and was open on one side.

Furniture from the Béarn was influenced by her Basque and Spanish neighbors. It is sturdy and powerful and is characterized by its so-called diamond-point carving, with designs made up of heavily incised straight lines. The Maltese cross was an early motif. Called a "besant," another feature was a convex disk carving based on a Byzantine coin. These disks or coins were carved in groups of four, surrounded by a quatrefoil and sometimes combined with other designs. Most of the pieces were of walnut and oak.

Now divided between Spain and France, the area of Catalonia originally was one. In the early days furniture of any kind was scarce and chests were the only storage piece. The ancient chests that have survived are Romanesque in design with round arches supported by columns on their facade.

In this region chests for men and chests for women were different. His had a double top, the outer one made of wood and the inner one covered with fabric. The chest was a showpiece, placed against the wall, often left with the outer cover open so that the inside showed. To further impress guests, the carving on the outside was repeated on the inside, a feature not found on chests of any other region. Her chest had only one top. The front was divided into panels, one of which was really a door. Behind this door was a set of shallow drawers intended for jewelry and other valuables. Clothes and linens were kept in the main part of the chest which opened from the top. The "bride's" chest was also decorated more simply than her husband's.

By the end of the eighteenth century, features of Louis XIII and Louis XV styles combined with existing Catalonian characteristics. A Catalonian characteristic is, for instance, a chest whose top is wider than the base, or painted pieces with a decidedly Spanish flavor. Decorated in religious themes, painted beds from this region with imposing headboards and painted armoires are great finds. Deep moldings are also found on armoires and cupboards.

History has not been kind to the Basques. They are a group united by language and culture, but divided for centuries by Spain and France. Most Basque pieces that interest furniture collectors are about one hundred and fifty years old. They reflect Hispano-Mauresque and French Basque characteristics. Two singular pieces, found nowhere else, come from this area: the "manka" and the "zuzulu." The manka is a two-door cupboard that looks like a low sideboard with a shallow chest on top. Sometimes the manka had a drawer at the bottom below the cupboard section, but only on later pieces. The zuzulu is a bench, long enough to seat three people, with a back in three sections, of which the middle one can be folded down to form a table.

Other Basque pieces are the chest, armoire, sideboard, tall buffet, and china dresser. The chest of drawers is not a Basque piece. Many pieces from this region are carved or have incised motifs. Many of these motifs can be found in the graveyards on old tombstones. Some of these designs are: scrolls, rosettes, wheels with whirling spokes, fans, crescent shapes known as commas, the sun, the moon, rays, and the swastika of Hindu origin. Crosses and geometric designs are important. Many Basque pieces are made of walnut, cherry, and wild cherry, with chestnut for the backs and perhaps the sides also.

Located near Paris, Brie was influenced by the sophisticated furniture of the capital. Fine eighteenth-century furniture can be found in this area. Even with the closeness of Paris the craftsmen of Brie developed furniture with a distinct character, the best-known piece being the "bahut briard," or Brie cupboard, now a sought-after piece by collectors. It has a shape found nowhere else in France—taller than the usual sideboard, but shorter than the average armoire.

Brie made its best furniture of oak. Eighteenth-century pieces are much finer than those made in the nineteenth century. Walnut was the second choice of the local craftsmen, and poplar was used for the least expensive pieces. These pieces often have what looks like a small fixed panel between two drawers that really conceals a secret compartment.

Furniture from Flanders shows the influences of Holland, the principality of Liège, Spain, and Italy. Early pieces are in the Gothic style. In the sixteenth century, Italian ideas were interpreted by the Flemish craftsmen. Pieces from this region are heavily ornamented. Five-door wardrobes were made in the region of Antwerp. Masks and cabochons are often found in the center of panels. Pilasters were decorated with caryatids. Gadrooned cornices have lion heads which were the emblem of Flanders. Busts with ribboned headdresses and motifs of the Virgin Mary and Neptune could be on the same piece. Baroque influences had little effect on the furniture of Flanders. Even before the end of the seventeenth century, Flemish cabinetmakers used twisted columns and exotic woods, particularly ebony. Veneering was a specialty of Flanders, often accented with ebony inlays. Chests were made for long-legged bases. The typical chest had two doors that opened to reveal a set of drawers and sometimes a tiny cupboard. The decorations on these cabinets were made of ebony, rosewood, ivory, tortoise-shell, and painted copper. These Flemish cabinets were the burgher's ultimate status symbol.

Another characteristic Flemish piece is the "ribbank." This is a four-door cupboard with the frame divided horizontally into two unequal sections. Its top is elbow height, but the long narrow doors of the shallow upper section are hinged at the bottom. Supported in a horizontal position, they can be used as a table. Extending beyond the piece, the cornice is heavily carved and usually contains two shallow drawers. The uprights are decorated with caryatids, busts on console, sprays of fruit, foliage and scrolls. These squat but massive pieces were supported on ball or claw feet. They were made of oak and were a rich man's piece.

Provence has furniture that was characteristically very interesting. During the sixteenth century, the Italian Renaissance style prevailed. From the beginning of the seventeenth century the influence "Frenchified," and furniture from Provence assumed a definite original personality incorporating Italian, French and local elements.

The area of Provence stretched northeast to the Comtat-Venaissin and radiated on the left bank of the Rhône to Bas-Dauphiné.

This furniture is usually solid, large, and has thick panels. The moldings are sturdy and have opulent lines. A graceful desk, the bureau de pente, has a parquetry lid.

Carving begins from Louis XVI and is more like engraving than carving. This carving appears only on the frames, not on the panels. The designs include flora, pine cones, olive branches, and sheaves of wheat and grapes.

Many pieces are constructed with swelled fronts, curved-in sides, S-shaped doors, and profiled cornices. In addition, there are round and fluted columns, some having turned or carved plumes and tassels. Various commodes have open carved, pierced aprons and cabriole legs. Commodes have two or three drawers.

Under Louis XV the decoration consisted mainly of moldings. Under Louis XVI there was carving. In the nineteenth century, decoration was overloaded on this furniture. Massive steel hinges were purposely made bigger than the furniture proportions indicated, and locks often covered the entire upright of a door.

Furniture from Normandy resembles that of Provence. Both have similar proportions and carving. However, Normandy is one of the rare places where the Empire style left an important imprint.

Marriage chests, commonly called "sailor's chests," were intended to be kept inside the big cupboard to hold small items. They were part of a bride's trousseau. Decorations usually consist of a solid-color background in blue, green, or ochre, usually with hearts, flowers, birds and ribbons. They were made between 1750 and 1850.

The armoire, usually with four doors and two drawers, is of somber construction with a molded cornice, often with a dentil border along the lower edge. The legs are short cabrioles in form with a scroll foot.

In Normandy, toward the end of the reign of Louis XIII and the beginning of that of Louis XIV, the chest gave way to the armoire.

The chimera motif is common on these Norman pieces. Various armoires have no drawers, but have beautifully carved cornices, perhaps with a wreath and love birds. A carved apron and additional carving surrounding the door panels might depict flowers or musical instruments. Medallions were another favorite design.

Arles is found at the tip of Provence. The great center of cabinetmaking was at Arles. A local piece from Arles is the buffet-credénce. It is a low buffet with scroll feet, closed by two wooden molding-covered doors, above which is a pair of drawers. On the top of this piece, to the rear, is a narrow second cupboard of equal length, with two small sliding doors in the front.

Another piece of furniture which is strictly provincial is the garde-manger or larder, which is a small narrow cupboard with one door in the center. The sides are spindled.

Early wardrobes were tall with double doors running from the bottom to the cornice. Under the Louis XIV influence the single door armoire was popular. This was preceded by the Louis XIII style with a two-storied, four-door wardrobe that was monumental in size. The wood used was mainly oak, but walnut, chestnut, and cherry were also used for these pieces. Eighteenth-century pieces often used olivewood moldings rather than carving.

Furniture from Catholic Arles is sober in form but richly decorated. Furniture from nearby Protestant Nimes is more exuberant in shape, but the furniture is similar. Designs based on wild flowers, roses, carnations, and tulips are found on these pieces. The "soup tureen" motif is found in various provinces and also on pieces from Arles and Nimes. Lovebirds might be carved below the cornice of armoires and a carved wheat-sheaf on the skirt.

Furniture from Guienne and Gascony, the two most southern provinces of France, are mainly in the Louis XIII style. This is the region with square armoires, heavy cornices, and doors decorated with diamond-point and cake-shaped insets. It is the region of double-bodied cabinets, the one above narrower than the one below, both supported by twisted columns. It is the region with chests carved with ornaments called "plumes." It is the area that made furniture in the Louis XIII style right up until the middle of the nineteenth century. Therefore, although it is in one style, it was not all made at the same time.

The region around Bordeaux is the only one in Gascony where the "royal styles" prospered during the seventeenth and eighteenth centuries, and the woods employed there were exotic and mostly imported.

Flanders, Artois, and Picardy form the northern border of France.

In Flanders, furniture was influenced by the Low Countries. The regional furniture is quite Dutch up to the seventeenth century with a Gothic tendency. The double-bodied armoires, called "ribbanks," are overloaded with carving. The pieces that succeeded them are covered with veneering, marquetry and inlay work. There is a taste for opulence even in simply ornamented pieces, which are often made of ebony and lightly but entirely carved.

One of the most characteristic pieces is a small, low armoire surmounted by a press with a hand screw, for pressing damp linen sheets.

Pieces from Artois and Picardy were often very unique. Some clung to their Gothic traditions, such as their chests and tables with X- and T-shaped legs.

Their wide armoires and buffets were comprised of two equally proportioned pieces, one above the other. The decoration on their four doors was usually diamond-point carving. Their buffets often had six doors, the center ones with a carved design different from the side doors.

A pannetière or bread box was in Louis XV style. It was rectangular and was hung on the wall. It opened by a spindled door in the middle.

The bas de buffet, with its pair of doors, each surmounted by a drawer, is common all over France, but in Artois and Picardy it is taller, standing five feet tall. On the other hand, another bas de buffet was also made, low and as wide as ten feet with four, five, or six doors. Then it was called a traite.

Another buffet had a paneled upper section and the lower section consisted of open racks for freshly washed dishes to drip. Some buffets had their center section comprised of drawers.

Furniture from Burgundy was greatly affected by the Renaissance. It was solidly built and opulent with elaborate carving. A characteristic piece is the small double-bodied cupboard, whose upper section is narrower than its main body and set back slightly. It was carved and embellished with human and allegorical figures. Feet on pieces from this area were often ball-shaped.

Liège was a city that always prized freedom and had often fought its city's rulers as well as outsiders. There, it was said "Even a poor man is a king in his own house." After Liège was annexed to Holland, the people revolted, which led to the establishment of Belgium, of which it has since been a part.

In the sixteenth century, Liège was a prosperous center and in the eighteenth century it reached a golden age. It had a powerful aristocracy and a rich bourgeoisie which required furniture.

Their cabinetmakers usually worked in oak but also used walnut. Their pieces were richly and delicately carved. They are luxurious but not flamboyant or ostentatious. Liège made elegant furniture.

The armoires were tall, often with four doors instead of two. Casepieces made in two sections are numerous. Clocks were sometimes set in the center, between the two pairs of doors on the upper section. A blackish tar was often applied to the furniture feet to protect them from dampness.

Motifs from the Louis XIV period are prevalent, many having ragged-edged shell carvings. Another detail was a cordonnet or rope, twisted into curves to form S and C shapes that wind around the edges of panels, doors, and drawers.

In addition to carved pieces, there were pieces decorated with geometric marquetry made with native woods such as walnut, boxwood, blackened pearwood, and elm burr. A few painted pieces constructed of ash wood are still in existence.

There are pieces from the region of Limousin that date from the 1100s. Like the region itself, they are rough and austere.

An oak armoire has been in the local church since about 1156. However, most furniture from this region dates from 1770 to 1850. Up into the nineteenth century, Limousin cabinetmakers built simple, severe, straight-lined furniture, decorated primarily with diamond shapes that were typical of Louis XIII's style. At the same time they also worked in the Louis XIV and Louis XV styles and even in the Louis-Philippe spirit. The Limousin also had excellent iron-mongers who made great andirons and fire-dogs which ornamented the hearth of local chateaus as well as those in the peasants' huts. Limousin pieces were made of oak, chestnut, elm, wild cherry, pear, and local fruit woods. Bourgeois pieces were more elaborate than peasant pieces, but not by much. There was a saying "The Limousin is poor in rich people." The dresser was the coveted status symbol in this region.

Furniture from the poor Morvan area is surprising. We could expect it to be austere because life was hard in this district. However, their pieces are cheerful and graceful with scalloped skirts, cambered feet, and panels whose moldings are attractively carved. They have simple decoration, sometimes carved only with a pocket-knife and compass. Whirling suns, swastikas, and geometric designs are found on these pieces. Morvan furniture is generally believed to be made exclusively of oak, but many pieces have oak combined with walnut, wild cherry, beech, and ash.

In Alsace, painted furniture was not bought by anyone who could afford better. Paint covered the defects in the cheap wood. Painted pieces went out of style about 1900. They were constructed of pine or fir by the local craftsmen as a substitute for carved hardwood pieces ordered by well-to-do patrons. When it was no longer wanted or needed, this furniture was given to the servants or burned for firewood. This is why it is rare and now valuable to collectors.

Alsatian furniture included tables, chairs, benches, and cupboards. Benches often have their owner's name inscribed on them. Sometimes religious inscriptions are found on these pieces. Early pieces often left the natural wood as the background, but more recent pieces of the late eighteenth century, were entirely painted.

Other motifs such as lozenges, five-pointed stars, six-pointed stars, rosettes, whirling sun designs, and many flowers, such as tulips, carnations, pansies, and daisies or bouquets were used to decorate this delightful furniture. The quatrefoil, acanthus, and foliated scroll were also used to decorate these pieces. Fake wood graining and mottling was also done, and many designs were stenciled. On more expensive pieces there were heavy moldings.

Early on, furniture from Touraine was constructed with high standards. It had two major characteristics: light-colored woods and restrained decoration. Oak was rarely used because it was considered too dark. People in this region preferred cherry, walnut, and pear. Applewood was also used in the Touraine region, but is rarely seen elsewhere. Therefore, if you see a simply decorated piece made of applewood, consider its origin the Touraine region.

Special characteristics of Tourangeau furniture can be observed on their armoires. The armoires were medium sized with sparse decoration that was usually confined to the moldings around the doors, consistently of one or two floral decorations. Touranqeau chairs often had scalloped slats. Four-poster beds were curtained to keep out drafts.

Brittany and La Bretogne produced simple boxy architectural pieces as well as exuberant, gracefully carved armoires. While many pieces had flat tops, others were double domed. These pieces were decorated with geometric symbols, flowers, spirals, swastikas, zigzags, grapes, and religious motifs. The roundel or circle was carved and also pierced with spindles. The apron often had a circular design in the center.

Enclosed beds, the lit-clos, were like small rooms, usually on straight legs with a flat top, often spindled and carved with religious symbols and flowers or geometric designs.

The garde-manger often had a pierced metal door.

A very fine blocked commode with short cabriole legs and fine hardware was made in this area.

When a girl married, she brought with her a chest, and after 1700, a wardrobe. On a painted piece, usually decorated with flowers, the bride's name and date were inscribed. These wardrobes could have one or two doors.

During the eighteenth century, a piece known as an "olmer" was made. It was multi-purpose and generally found in the kitchen. It was a combination closet, larder, china cabinet, and chest of drawers. It was a large piece and was sometimes incorporated into a paneled wall.

You can see how the furniture of various areas differed. Its characteristics, woods, and decorations indicate where it originated.

REGIONAL CHARACTERISTICS

Alsace Known for painted pieces. Pine and fir woods. Rare. The owner's name with a date often inscribed on wardrobes. Motifs include five- and six-pointed stars, rosettes drawn with a compass, whirling suns, flowers, and bouquets.

Arles Large, solid, thick paneled furniture. Carving sometimes more like engraving. Various casepieces have swelled fronts and curved-in sides. Pierced aprons are common. Armoires often eight feet tall. Furniture from Catholic Arles is sober in form but richly decorated. Motifs include the "soup-tureen" and "love-birds."

Artois X- and T-shaped legs. A singular kitchen piece made of two small one-door cupboards with a long central niche between them fitted with shelves. Glazed china cabinets (vitrines) influenced by Flemish designs. Motifs include urns, stars, and diamonds. Cherry and oak were favored woods.

Basque Spanish influences. Singular pieces are the manka and zuzulu. The chest of drawers is not a Basque piece. Geometric designs are important. The Basque dresser has a top display section as deep as the cupboard below. Armoires are tall and slim. Woods include walnut, cherry, and wild cherry.

Béarn Influenced by Basque and Spanish neighbors. Sturdy. Often of walnut and oak woods. Broken arch pediments are seen on various casepieces. Feet are scrolled, squared, and bun. Motifs include the Maltese cross, disk shapes, crisscross, and the diamond-point. Flowers, hearts, and birds were also local favorites.

Burgundy Solidly built, opulent carving, human allegorical figures, ball feet. Walnut important.

Brie Influenced by Parisian craftsmen. Sideboard taller than usual, but shorter than average armoire. It is known as a "three-quarter" or "square" cupboard. Best pieces constructed of oak and walnut. Wild flowers, slim foliage sprays, wheat and shell motifs are important.

Brittany Boxy, simple, architectural. Graceful armoires. Flat or double-domed tops on casepieces. Aprons often have centered circular design or a circular spindle.

Catalonia Spanish and Romanesque influences. Different chests for men and women. Chests with the top wider than the base are found here. Deep moldings. Painted beds are important. Small armoires were used to store linens. Pomegranates, symbol of plenty, were found on bridal chests.

Chalosse Chalosse lies north of Béarn. Armoires display sharply incised carving. Criss-cross decorations often appear, as do shells, fans and sprays. The dove is a frequent motif. The "half-armoire," half as wide, was made here. Woods used were oak, chestnut, wild cherry, pine, and poplar.

Charente Fine marquetry work. Dark highlights brushed with indelible ink. Motifs include diamond-point carving, stars, Maltese crosses. Saw-tooth borders. Large mounts. Woods include walnut, cherry, wild cherry, and elm.

Dauphiné Pellet feet (flattened roll), swelled-front casepieces, fine marquetry, inlay, some rococo carving. Motifs include floral forms, acanthus leaves, and foliage scrolls. Also a narrow black fillet for accent.

Flanders Dutch and Gothic influences up to seventeenth century. Double-bodied armoires. Carving, veneering, marquetry and inlay work. Ebony inlays notable. Straight, bun, and claw feet. Five-door wardrobes are typical of this region.

Masks and cabochons are seen in middle of panels. The "lion of Flanders" appears on some armoires. Oak widely used. Many ornate pieces.

Gascony and Guienne   The two southern-most provinces. Square armoires, heavy cornices. Doors often inset with diamond-point carving. Sides often made of cheaper woods. A long chest of drawers with an armoire on top was made here.

Liège   Richly and delicately carved. Four-door armoires. Louis XIV styles important. Ragged-edge shell carving and rope carving edged panels. Geometric marquetry. Oak and walnut.

Limousin   Austere pieces. Straight lined, simple construction. Diamond shape important for decoration. Romanesque style of architecture reflected in furniture. Oak, chestnut, elm, and wild cherry woods used. A dresser with a cut-out base made to hold a soup-tureen is probably from Limousin.

Lyons   Somber. Rather heavy. Armoires may be nine feet tall. Deeply cut moldings. Walnut favored.

Morvan   Graceful scalloped skirts. Motifs include whirling suns, swastikas, geometric shapes. Shallow carving of a flower bouquet below the cornice of an armoire. Usual woods were walnut, wild cherry, and poplar. Toward end of nineteenth century, factory-made furniture in Empire or Louis-Philippe styles were made of walnut veneers.

Nantes   Walnut was originally the prized wood but mahogany became important beginning in 1722. More furniture was made of mahogany in Nantes than in any other French port city. Nantes pieces reflect the Paris styles beginning with Louis XIV. A local piece was the "cabaret," a little table with a slightly hollowed-out top. Another piece was a cylinder-top desk inspired by Louis XV designs. Some casepieces have flat tops and others an arch or double arch. Various pieces have panels bordered with slightly waved moldings.

Scrolled feet and bun feet are evident. Aprons are often scalloped.

Normandy Early pieces reflect Italian influence. Empire designs very important. Various armoires have no drawers but have beautifully carved cornices, often with a wreath or love-birds.

Provence Sixteenth-century pieces reflect the Italian Renaissance. Beginning in the seventeenth century, Italian and French elements merged. Similar pieces from Normandy.

Rouergue Louis XIII shapes are important here. Straight lines, straight or ball feet, and straight or round molding frame the flat panels on which inlays are placed. Inlay motifs included birds and flowers such as the iris, tulip, and poppy. Geometric motifs are seen on later pieces. Door panels are cut into lozenges called "double X's." A six-door buffet is typical of Rouergue. An armoire with a triangular pediment is probably from Rouergue.

Touraine Graceful pieces. Fruitwoods preferred. Medium-sized, sparse decoration usually confined to moldings around doors. Sideboards with deeply scalloped skirts and S-shaped feet ending in a scroll. Chairs often have scalloped slats. Feet squared, scrolled, and bun. The daisy is a favorite motif.

Toulouse This province avoided oak, preferring local fruitwoods and grey paint. Influenced by nearby Spain. Favorite carved motif was fluting. Marquetry made by Dutch craftsmen. A Louis XVI slant-top desk with fluting is typical of Toulouse.

AUCTION TERMS

An auction is a public sale where property goes to the highest bidder.

Today we have a global auction market; however, particular pieces sell differently in various parts of the country or the world.

The auction house owns no property; it is the agent providing a service to the seller and buyer.

Services can be negotiated!

Check with more than one auction house.

Larger auction houses have separate departments for furniture, paintings, etc., that have an expert in charge of each. Each department produces catalogues and handles sales. You can write or phone an auction house requesting particular catalogues or specific sale information. There is a charge for catalogues. You can also subscribe to catalogues. You can request price (digests) sheets listing what each particular piece in the sale sold for. There is also a charge for this service.

Auction viewing rooms are good places to see, handle, and learn about furniture. Treat yourself to hours of pleasure before the sale in the category you are most interested in.

The private collector has the edge over the dealer who must buy at a price that enables him to sell at a profit.

The commission to the house is called a "buyer's premium."

There is also a "seller's premium."

An absentee or pocket bid is an offer left in person, or by mail, with the auctioneer before the sale. The record of absentee bids is kept by the house and given the same recognition as bids made during the actual sale. The record of an absentee bid is termed "book."

Be sure you know what the piece you bid on looks like. Take notes when you view it. The house will allow you to handle the piece under supervision before the sale at a "viewing time." Note distinguishing marks, cracks, colors, scratches, etc.

A "switch" is the substitution of a piece originally on view, for one of a lower value prior to or after the sale.

If you cannot be present at a particular auction and are hesitant to offer an absentee bid without viewing the piece or pieces, many dealers will bid for you. They should agree to phone you after examining the object in order to describe the condition. Then, if you wish, they will bid for you at an agreed-on price. You will pay a commission to the dealer in addition to the one you pay the house. Only contact dealers that handle this particular type of object and who will be attending the auction to buy for themselves. You do not want a dealer who is not familiar with the type of piece you plan to bid on.

"As is" is an auction term meaning the article is in some way damaged and will be sold in that condition.

A "reserve" is the lowest price agreed on by the seller and the house beneath which the article cannot be sold. The seller will take the article back if that price is not reached.

An "unreserved auction" means there is no reserve and the article goes to the highest bidder no matter how low the last bid is.

A "hidden reserve" is a reserve agreed upon by the seller and the house, unknown to the bidder.

Auction catalogues often give an estimate for each item. Example: $1,000 to $1,500. *The $1,000 is not the reserve.* If you want to leave an absentee bid, perhaps offer 70 percent of the low estimate or $700.

"Chandelier bids" or "phantom bids" are false bids used by auctioneers to increase genuine bidding at sales.

A "pool" is a clutch of bidders, not necessarily dealers, who attempt to restrain or force up bidding for their personal profit.

A "ring" is a group of people, usually dealers, who gather together to cheat the house and the seller by keeping the bidding between themselves if possible, and keeping it low. After acquiring an object or objects, the "ring" may then hold another auction among themselves to divide the goodies.

Do not pass up auctions that don't specialize in the furniture you collect. You may find just what you are searching for, at a reasonable price, hidden among the featured furniture. For example, if you collect Louis XV furniture, you might find an isolated Louis XV piece available at an auction billed as featuring "Empire furniture," for a much lower price than would be the case if other Louis XV collectors were bidding against you.

Call an auction house after a sale to see if unsold pieces are available below the original reserve. You would still be responsible for the auction house commission. Individual auction house policies would dictate any possible procedure. The owner of any piece in question would have to be consulted and would have to agree before a post-auction sale.

COLLECTING AND BUYING

Collecting and buying is what antique lovers do best. Our adventures keep the adrenaline flowing. I may never work out on an exercise bike, but when the occasion arises, I can run up three flights of crooked stairs in an antique warehouse. Why? Because it is exciting to search for treasure. A cave man after a wild boar could not compete with some of my fellow antique hunters.

Forming a collection is a creative process. Collectors are free to assemble their collections with any combinations they choose. Often the most individual combinations form the most exciting collections. A collection does not necessarily require every known example of period designs, and often can be equally interesting when assembled within tight limits. A totally eclectic mix pleases many collectors. Like a "driver," the collector picks the route. You may also consider combining more than one collection, such as French period furniture and African masks, Oriental rugs, or a modern art collection.

Whether we are purchasing a few pieces, building a collection, or furnishing our homes with antique French furniture, "a great find" is always our goal. We may not get all we desire, but why not give it a good try?

French furniture is scarce compared to English furniture. More legwork is required unless you live in New Orleans or New York. Recently an American George Nelson sofa from 1956 sold for $16,500. That week, however, I stumbled over an exquisite Louis XV painted settee for $11,500. Expensive yes, but of great value! What surprises me are the prices that collectibles are going for: A comic book for $55,000, or a baseball shirt worn by Mickey Mantle for $71,500. It is a question of what you value. I will take the settee and two eighteenth-century cane chairs.

With intelligent and diligent pursuit, it is possible to acquire antique French furniture for the price of fine new reproductions. Antique French furniture will always be an investment and French pieces are very special.

I am convinced that it is unnecessary to settle for reproductions when period pieces, or "in the style of" furniture from the nineteenth century are available. Many auction houses have sales featuring Continental and French nineteenth-century furniture. Many of these pieces are well made, beautiful, and go for less than fine new reproductions. With the antique piece you get period design, tradition, and a softer look, perhaps from a provincial home. The purchaser can also turn around and sell antique furniture at the next auction and probably make a profit.

French furniture is for sale in the Chicago area as well as in New York, New Orleans, Dallas, Seattle, and Washington, D.C. Check advertisements in home furnishing magazines. If you see an advertisement featuring furniture you are interested in, pick up the phone and call. Ask for photographs. You might decide to take a trip.

New Orleans, Louisiana, is a must for lovers of French furniture. There are many shops, auction houses, and historic homes open to the public. Toronto is a similar treasure trove.

Working with a dealer can be a tremendous help. They can network to locate exactly what you are searching for. Most dealers will put themselves out for a good customer.

If you use a decorator, be sure they know French antique furniture. Many do not have sufficient knowledge. Any piece you buy should have a complete description and price under a letterhead.

Facilities "to the trade only" may allow you access if you carry a letter from a retail source where a bill can be sent.

I caution against large investments at antique shows that are not vetted. I frequent many antique shows that contain suspect pieces and basically secondhand merchandise. It comes down to how familiar you are with antique French furniture. Do not mix liquor and shopping. Many shows serve "refreshments."

Antique furniture has entered the office place. French desks, cabinets, and chairs are impressive. They are a deductible business expense and, when you retire, they can come home with you or go to auction for your retirement savings. My husband recently refurnished his office. All the old furniture sold for about $300. He had originally paid more for the desk alone.

You must be prepared for the possibility of forgeries. I hope that after reading the chapter on clues, you will have a better understanding of faking.

It is always prudent to buy from established dealers who constantly handle French antique furniture, and who buy from reputable sources. I recently was called in to see a problem table that had been bought on a vacation in Europe. I am sorry to say that my best advice was to get rid of it.

Perception and current tastes change, but the furniture itself remains the same. Twenty-five years ago Napoleon III furniture was not generally appreciated. Today some of these pieces are more expensive than earlier eighteenth century ones. If you buy what reflects your individual taste, you will reap the best reward. Let's go over options for acquiring antique French furniture.

1. Inherit.

2. Retail—Dealers will often allow you to try a piece in your home. They usually require payment in full, but will immediately destroy your check if the piece is returned.

3. Auction houses—Have you ever attended a "viewing" where the items can be inspected? Catalogues are very important reading because they suggest prices and provide descriptions. If you bid, be sure you can identify the item. Note cracks, patina, mounts, or any distinguishing marks. If you can't attend the actual auction, consider a "closed" or "pocket" bid. I believe in leaving "absentee bids." You may be happily surprised when you are "the winner." If you do attend, *set a realistic price above which you will not go.* Remember, you will also pay a buyer's premium. It is a practical idea to subscribe to catalogues featuring antique French furniture. They are excellent reference material.

4. House sales—If you have a good eye and a working knowledge of antique furniture, bargains may exist. Maybe your name is on a French cabinet. Even if the furniture is disappointing, perhaps you will find a sterling cake server, an iron garden seat, or an art glass treasure.

5. Newspaper advertisements—Be sure the advertiser really owns the property. I answered an advertisement where I am sure the pieces were not the property of the advertiser.

6. Antiques class—Consider taking a class in antiques. Some are offered at high schools and colleges. Are there any antique clubs in your area? They very often have knowledgeable guest speakers.

In Paris, the Louvre Antiquaries at 2 pl du Palais Royal, with 250 dealers, is a treat. Also, Village Suisse at 78 Avenue de Suffren, five blocks from the Hilton, offers a fine choice of furniture and French antiques.

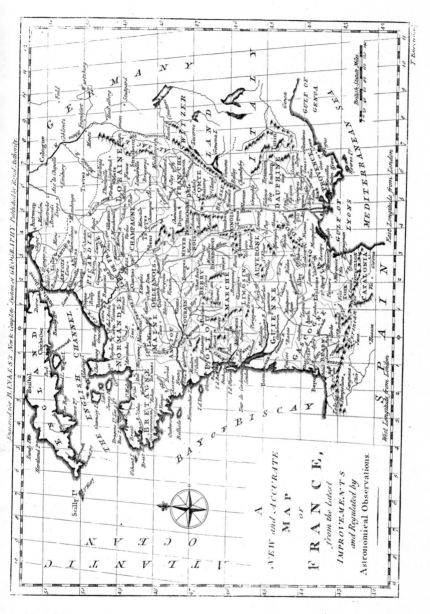

Map of France, circa 1780.
Courtesy of Jeanne Siegel.

Various design elements.
Courtesy of Seng Handbook

Directory-Consulate-period chair. Crosier back, palm leaf carving, tacked upholstery on seat and back.
Courtesy of Jeanne Siegel.

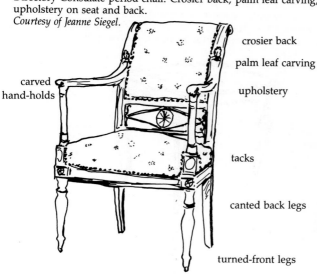

crosier back

palm leaf carving

carved hand-holds

upholstery

tacks

canted back legs

turned-front legs

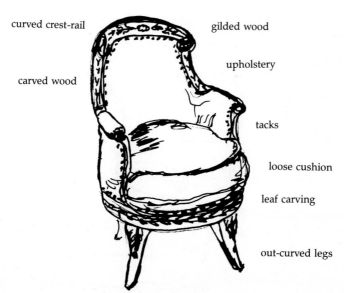

curved crest-rail

gilded wood

upholstery

carved wood

tacks

loose cushion

leaf carving

out-curved legs

Empire chair from the nineteenth century. Carved and gilded wood, upholstered with removable cushion, slightly curved legs. Note the resemblance to the earlier Italian gondola chair.
Courtesy of Jeanne Siegel.

Louis XV ormolu-mounted parquetry table à écrire. The rectangular quarter-veneered top has a serpentine shape that is surrounded by an ormolu border. The frieze is fitted with one drawer. The cabriole legs are decorated with ormolu chutes as well as ormolu C scrolls and foliage on the upper part of each leg. *Courtesy of Jeanne Siegel.*

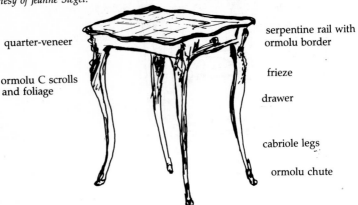

quarter-veneer

serpentine rail with ormolu border

ormolu C scrolls and foliage

frieze

drawer

cabriole legs

ormolu chute

Louis XV giltwood bergère, mid-eighteenth century. Displays serpentined rails, a centered flower head in the top-rail, and fine carvings. The armrests are padded, it has a serpentine-fronted seat, cabriole legs, and scrolled toes. *Courtesy of Jeanne Siegel.*

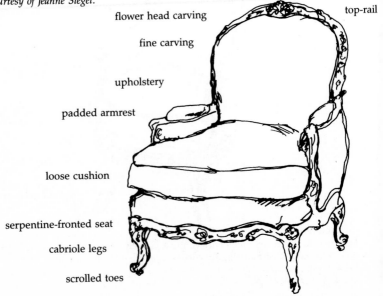

flower head carving

top-rail

fine carving

upholstery

padded armrest

loose cushion

serpentine-fronted seat

cabriole legs

scrolled toes

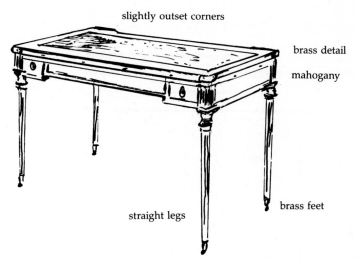

slightly outset corners

brass detail

mahogany

straight legs

brass feet

Directoire tric-trac table, circa 1800. Mahogany, brass detail, lid lifts to reveal a backgammon board.
Courtesy of Jeanne Siegel.

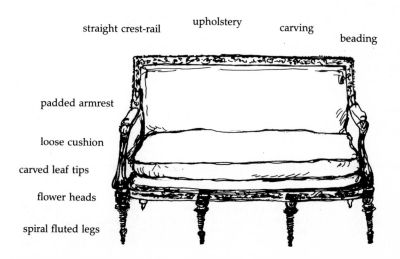

straight crest-rail

upholstery

carving

beading

padded armrest

loose cushion

carved leaf tips

flower heads

spiral fluted legs

Eighteenth-century painted canapé. Features leaf-tip and laurel garland carvings, beading, spiral fluted legs with carved flower heads, upholstered seat and back, loose cushion, and padded armrests.
Courtesy of Jeanne Siegel.

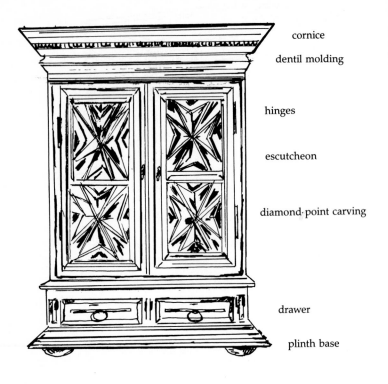

cornice

dentil molding

hinges

escutcheon

diamond-point carving

drawer

plinth base

bun feet

bail mount

Louis XIII massive cupboard. Features a heavy cornice, flattened bun feet, doors with bold geometric carving, and two drawers in the bottom portion. *Courtesy of Jeanne Siegel.*

Sixteenth-century Renaissance buffet with solid wood carving, figures in ovals, stylized flora, acanthus leaves, marble inlay, and bun feet. Features an architectural pediment with a statuette, Italian influence. *Courtesy of Jeanne Siegel.*

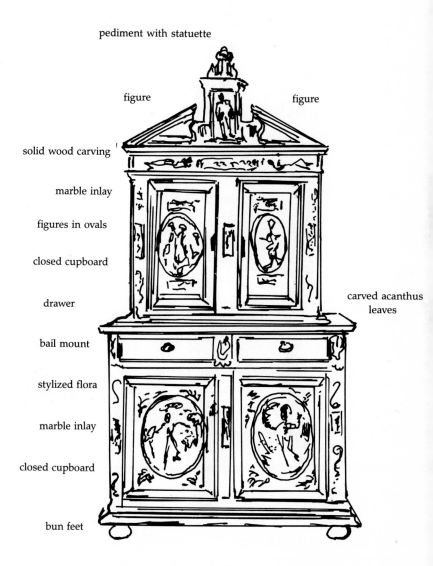

pediment with statuette

figure   figure

solid wood carving

marble inlay

figures in ovals

closed cupboard

drawer

bail mount

stylized flora

marble inlay

closed cupboard

bun feet

carved acanthus leaves

Louis XVI fauteuil à la reine.
Courtesy of William Doyle Galleries, New York, New York.

Louis XVI mahogany and tulipwood table à écrire.
Courtesy of William Doyle Galleries, New York, New York.

Pair of Louis XV walnut fauteuils en cabriolet from the mid-eighteenth century.
Courtesy of William Doyle Galleries, New York, New York.

Settee made from satinwood and abalone-inlaid rosewood. Features a scrolled
inlaid crest with gilt highlights and cabriole legs. In the Aubusson style, it is from
the last quarter of the nineteenth century.
Courtesy of Leslie Hindman Auctioneers, Chicago, Illinois.

Louis XVI-style console table from the late nineteenth century. Features a marble top, a carved gesso and giltwood frieze in relief, fluted tapered legs with an acanthus motif, and a demi-lune shape.
Courtesy of Leslie Hindman Auctioneers, Chicago, Illinois.

Louis XV-style tulipwood and kingwood commode.
Courtesy of William Doyle Galleries, New York, New York.

Louis XVI dining table with brass detail and casters.
Courtesy of William Doyle Galleries, New York, New York.

Early nineteenth-century provincial cherry wood table. Features cabriole legs and a scalloped apron.
Courtesy of the Antique Emporium, Winnetka, Illinois.

Pair of Louis XVI gray-painted fauteuils à medaillon.
Courtesy of William Doyle Galleries, New York, New York.

Louis XVI walnut canapé à corbeille. Finely carved, this piece is upholstered with
a loose, tacked cushion and a serpentine back.
Courtesy of William Doyle Galleries, New York, New York.

Pine armoire with a curved cornice, cabriole legs, carved floral motifs, and a scalloped apron. From eighteenth-century Normandy.
Courtesy of The Antique Emporium, Winnetka, Illinois.

Louis XVI provincial fruitwood dressing table.
Courtesy of William Doyle Galleries, New York, New York.

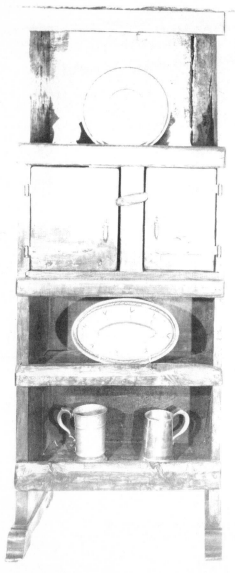

Chestnut vassilier, circa 1800.
Courtesy of the Antique Emporium, Winnetka, Illinois.

SELLING

While acquiring antiques we love is a pleasure, disposing of them can be troublesome. The treasure often becomes a mere object. DO NOT IGNORE THE CHALLENGING ADVENTURE OF SELLING. The value of stock investments are determined on the day they are sold. Antiques give pleasurable dividends while you live with them but also give a good return on investment when intelligently sold. Antique French furniture has long been a very good investment.

You have choices when you decide to part with your possessions. DO NOT SETTLE FOR AN INADEQUATE PRICE FROM A LOCAL SHOP JUST TO GET THE PIECE OR PIECES OUT OF THE HOUSE. Someone worked to get the best price when the piece was acquired. Do not be content with less than the best price when you sell. French furniture, especially if "of the period," should command a high price. Later in this chapter I will discuss what to do when you inherit an estate.

You cannot sell effectively if you have no idea of the "market value" of your antiques. Look in shops carrying similar antiques, go to antique shows, check with an appraiser, or call in an auction house. I have gone to homes to appraise one piece and said "What about that one?" The reply was, "That old thing?" That particular old thing was worth a small lottery prize. At the very least, look at current price guides. Consider your options carefully. DO NOT BE LAZY. Selling wisely puts the money in YOUR POCKET where it belongs.

Even if you think something is ugly, it is not necessarily valueless. At a recent auction, a pair of "ugly" old cups sold for $2,500 and an "ugly" picture for six figures.

I have found that many senior citizens love to realize the profit on their belongings themselves. Some to prove that they were smart when they acquired the pieces, or for the stimulation of participating in a sale, or because they could use the money for their living expenses. Sometimes damaged pieces make their owners believe that they are worthless. This is false! Antiques can be restored and retain their value.

It is very important for senior citizens to have their possessions appraised before it becomes too much of an effort. Many valuable items are lost, which is sad, and their owners lose their cash value, which is also sad.

Heirs unknowingly may dispose of valuable pieces. (It is very French to save or not give away what can be sold). Sometimes the children of older parents are forced to take over. Most try hard and mean well, but are themselves often stressed out and overworked. In many instances sentimental value works out fine, as when the grandchildren ask for the furniture, but not always. If the parents or other relatives need additional funds, selling may be the solution. Recently French gilt candlesticks sold for $25,000, a Louis XV-style tall case clock for $7,500, French posters in the thousands of dollars, a Galle vase for $15,400, a Régence-style canapé for $4,950, a 1925 torchere for $9,350, and a set of Louis XVI painted fauteuils for $49,000.

Auctions are an option, a good option! Do you have an auction house nearby? Call their consignment department. They will put you in touch with an expert dealing with your type of item, or they will even send an expert out to your home if necessary. Ask questions. Check with more than one auction house to see which one will do the most for you. *YOU CAN NEGOTIATE!* Ask what promotion they will give your piece or collection (request a photograph in the catalogue) and what services are available. Ask about packing, shipping, and payment. Do you want a reserve? Will there be a seller's premium?

If you are not near an auction house, write to one or more. Describe your piece or collection, enclose a sharp photograph and a copy of your original bill of sale if you have kept it. You will hear from them; auction houses are good about getting back to potential clients.

If you believe you have a rare piece or collection, I would suggest only major auction houses. Be sure your item will be in a sale of similar objects, insuring many bidders.

Another choice is to offer it back to the original place of purchase. Most antique dealers are delighted to recover an old piece they have already researched and profitably sold. You might make a deal for cash, or the dealer might take it on a consignment basis or take your piece in trade for a different piece. I hope you have saved the original invoice. *Any transaction should be in writing.*

Consignment means allowing a dealer to sell on your behalf for a percentage of the sale price. (You own the object until it is sold.) *If you put the piece on consignment, get the terms in writing.* The terms agreed upon should be on the shop's letterhead, dated and signed. Deal only with a person you trust to inform you of the price actually received. Only leave your piece at a shop that has a fast turnover. Otherwise, it could sit until you are nearly as old as the antique.

If a friend wants to purchase a piece from you, have it appraised first. Then both of you know the market value and can agree on a fair price.

Disposing of an entire estate is a problem many people face. It is emotionally draining and physically exhausting. A tremendous amount of sorting is necessary. I recommend keeping a notebook where you can list the items as you sort through them. Keep separate pages for glass, china, furniture, art work, and so on. When you do the bookcases, check for first editions and illustrated books. Children's books such as the Oz series bring great prices. Separate historical material such as military papers, deeds, stock certificates, union cards, school report cards, and even old library cards. Some have value in money and others for family history. Certain pieces might be valued by local historical societies. These might give you a write-off and also you have the satisfaction of knowing that they are not lost. Check old letters for their stamps and for historic importance. Keep the envelopes intact. I realize it is tempting to just dump bags of old things in the garbage, especially if you live out of town, but try to sort through them.

It is tempting to simply have a house sale and be done with the problem. Still, I hope you will hire an appraiser first, if only to pick out the most valuable pieces that you may want to keep.

Donations can be a fast route if you need a tax write-off, so check with your accountant. In 1991, the government began allowing museum donations at "market value." Some charities will provide you with a receipt indicating value that will be acceptable to the Internal Revenue Service.

Classified advertisements are an alternate choice. Are you willing to allow strangers into your home? If not, a small piece might be shown at your bank where they have special private rooms.

Everything is worth something to someone.

Whatever arrangements you make, consider the physical welfare of the piece or collection. Whenever or however you dispose of your antiques by sale or gift, be sure they remain in good condition and in good hands. Everything in life is lent to us and we, in turn, should see that our possessions will be available to future generations. That is the moral responsibility of the antique collector or inheritor.

FRENCH FURNITURE VOCABULARY

A la grecque Classic Greek style. Examples in the Directoire and Empire periods.

Acanthus A leaf design. The acanthus was a wild plant native to Southern Europe. Its beautiful, ragged leaves were an important decorative detail on columns in the Classical period of Greece and Rome. The Renaissance revived this leaf design. Examples are carved on furniture made during the reign of Henry II. Scrolled, acanthus leaf-carved stretchers are found on Louis XIV console tables. Also on Régence sabots, their edges outlined in ormolu.

Accent panel A wood inlay of a contrasting wood usually in geometric shape.

Alabaster A granular variety of gypsum.

All original A piece that has all the parts it was born with, except for very small repairs.

Ambry An English medieval cupboard, could be free-standing or built into an existing wall. Those with pierced doors were usually for food storage. Also used in churches for sacred vessels. The French word is armoire.

Ameublement Furniture.

Amorini Winged cupids, gods of love or carved cherubs.

Aniline Term applied to dyes derived from coal tar. Used to decorate fabrics after discovery in 1856. These dyes resulted in many rainbow hues.

Antefix   An upright ornament.

Anthemion   A Greek honeysuckle or chamomile foliage design.

Antimacassar   A nineteenth-century doily used in the Napoleon III and Victorian period to protect chair backs from soiling, because hair at that time was dressed with macassar oil.

Applied cresting   A carved ornament attached to uppermost furniture elements such as the top-rail of a chair or sofa.

Applied decoration   A separate added piece. An example is the spindle glued on medieval chests.

Applied molding   A molding, often geometric, applied to the face of furniture to create a panelled effect. Examples on provincial pieces in the eighteenth century.

Appliqué   This is often an additional decoration, usually applied with glue.

Appraisal   The worth of a piece, valued by an expert and usually done in writing. It is often used for insurance, potential sale, or settling an estate.

Apron piece   A skirt between the legs of the seat-frame of a chair or between the legs of a casepiece. Louis XV commodes had shaped aprons with ormolu mounts.

Arabesque   Decorative scrollwork or other intricate ornament composed of foliage, leaves and fruit, or fantastic animals or figures.

Arcaded back   An arch back. A furniture back with an arcade design between the top-rail and the seat. Arched backs are seen on early medieval Gothic pieces.

Arched aperture   An arched opening.

Arched skirt   Also called an arched or arcaded apron. An apron designed with arcade shapes that may be round or pointed. Many provincial pieces have arched skirts.

Arched stretchers   Arched stretchers are arc or hoop shaped.

Arches   Arches on furniture are usually round (Roman) or pointed (Gothic).

Architectural furniture   Furniture in which the design includes architectural characteristics such as paneling, usually in the form of large pieces. Examples of this are medieval chests, chairs, and structural corner cupboards.

Arm pads   This is partial upholstery on the arms of chairs and sofas. Examples on Louis XVI pieces.

Arm stump   This is also called an arm support. It is the vertical piece which supports the front of a chair arm.

Armoire   A large wardrobe or moveable cupboard with shelves and one or more doors.

Armoire à deux   Tall cupboard, front and sides of upper body recessed, lower section more oblong. Examples in Louis XIII period.

Art Nouveau   (1875–1914) This style is characterized by curvilinear motifs derived from natural forms, highly influenced by whiplash lines seen in Japanese prints. This design used Gothic and Japanese shapes. Henri Van de Velde and Emil Galle were outstanding designers of this style. The typical line is long and slightly curved, ending in a whip-like sharp curve. This style was most important in France. (English Art Nouveau was never as stylized as French and Belgium designs.)

Astrogel molding   A convex bead molding often used to overlap the joining of double doors.

Athénien   Athenian. From Athens.

Athénienne   Small decorative stand or table in the form of an antique Pompeiian tripod.

Back stool   Form of stool with a back developed in the sixteenth century. Also an early name for an upholstered side chair.

Backsplash   A decorative backboard attached to a sideboard or wash stand flanking the wall, ostensibly to protect the wall from splashed food or water. Some have side elements like galleries.

Bail   A half-loop metal pull hanging down from a metal plate. May be called a drop handle.

Baize   A woolen fabric resembling felt, usually green, found on the tops of some game tables.

Ball-and-claw foot   Associated with English and American furniture. A foot with a dragon or eagle claw holding a pearl or ball. This design originated in the Orient.

Ball foot   A boldly turned foot in the shape of a ball. Examples on buffets. Circa 1580.

Ball turnings   Turnings of closely spaced balls. Examples on various fauteuils in Louis XIII period. Back legs not turned.

Baluster   A small, slender turning usually with a square base. These may be in a vase shape. Short, carved baluster legs are found on Louis XVI beds in a vase shape.

Bamboo   The hollow woody stem of the genus Bambusa.

Bamboo turnings   Turnings simulating bamboo. Ormolu supports (legs) designed to resemble real bamboo are found on Louis XVI tables with Sèvres porcelain tops and side plaques. Real bamboo was used in various Napoleon III pieces.

Banding   A band of colored inlay contrasting with the surrounding surface.

Banister back   Vertical banisters that are set or mortised into the crest and bottom rail of chairs.

Banisters   Also called "balusters." They are semi-circular spindles.

Banquettes   A wall seat. Examples in the Louis XVI period.

Baracan   A ribbed worsted cloth.

Baroque   Extravagant designs developed principally in Italy and Western Europe during the seventeenth and early eighteenth centuries. Irregularly-shaped pieces with fantastic conspicuous curves and broken scrolls. Influence seen on rococo pieces.

Bas d' Armoire   A low cupboard, usually rectangular, surmounted by a marble slab. May have one or two doors.

Base   The horizontal element on casepieces immediately above the feet or the bottom of a column.

Base molding   Applied molding around the base of a casepiece.

Batten   A strip of wood used to cover joints between boards.

Bead molding   Small semi-circular molding.

Bearer   The rectangular section under a bureau fall which pulls out to support the fall when open.

Bell flower   A stylized flower with a narrow cup shaped with a flaring mouth and three to five clappers (petals).

Bench-carving   A piece made separately and applied.

Bench end   The upright end of a church pew.

Bergamot   A coarse tapestry used in the sixteenth century.

Bergère   A chair with filled insides. Might have wings. Early bergères were carved and later ones were upholstered. Examples in Régence period. A French word used to describe Louis XV-style closed armchairs. A less common English word to describe this piece is a barjier.

Berseil   A low cradle. Examples in Louis XIV period.

Bevel   A slanting, cutting away of an edge.

Bibliothèque   A bookcase.

Bine   The raised part of a spiral turning.

Biomorphic splat design   Splat with shapes evoking images of biological organisms without representing any specific organisms. Usually used to describe splats having a Rococo style.

Bird's-eye   Small brown markings resembling a bird's eye seen on maple timbers.

Blackamoor   An African figure used as the carved central sections of Louis XIV guéridons.

Blaze   Another name for a flame or corkscrew finial.

Blind doors   Solid doors, often double, that conceal small drawers or compartments.

Block   A square element, topping front legs, often with a centered concentric design.

Block foot   A foot shaped like a cube.

Block front pieces   The center recedes in a flattened curve while the end curves outward in a flattened bulge.

Blocks   Structural element used for bracing.

Board chest   A chest constructed by nailing boards together to form a rectangular chest. Board chests were not as strong as panel chests. Nails, not dowels, were used on board chests.

Bobbin turning   A turning resembling a wound bobbin. A provincial detail.

Bois d'ébénisterie   Wood used by cabinetmakers.

Bois durci   Name given to imitation ebony carvings (of French manufacture) that were introduced in England during the Victorian period. Bois durci carvings were used to ornament ebonized cabinets and were in the shape of Grecian heads, rosettes, and paterna forms.

Bolection molding   A raised molding having flat edges and a raised center.

Bombé   Furniture with a rounded front, a convex shape. Examples in eighteenth century of a rustic secretaire (secretary) with a bombé shape. Bracket feet on these pieces often match. Commodes of the Louis XV period have the bombé shape. The English imitated these pieces.

Bonheur du jour   A small writing table. May have an addition of a paper rack and drawers. Could also be a feminine bureau with tambour doors, a gallery, a writing lid, and four slender legs. Examples in Louis XVI period.

Bonnetière   A tall narrow cupboard with a long panelled door first seen in Louis XIV period. Many sheltered ladies' bonnets.

Bookcase Bookcases, either fitted or contained in other furniture, were known from medieval times.

Bordello furniture Includes pieces like a siège d'amour (love chair), which was made in the rococo style.

Boss A round or egg shaped ornament that was glued on.

Bottle turning A turned detail of Dutch origin, so called because of its resemblance to a bottle.

Boucle Indicates a curled nap on fabric.

Bouillotte table A Louis XVI game table for the game of bouillotte.

Boule A commode having fine boulle work.

Boulle work Type of marquetry using tortoise shell and metal. Perfected by André-Charles Boulle in eighteenth-century France. The process originated in Italy in the tenth century.

Bourgeois Middle class.

Bow top A chair top-rail with one low, unbroken curve across its width.

Bowl turnings Broader than a cup turning.

Box settle A medieval chest or box that functioned as a seat, often with a straight back.

Box stretcher Stretchers that form a rectangle.

Bracket Reinforcement of the angle between parts or surfaces on a piece of furniture. A shaped bracket reinforces the joining of a leg to the seat rail of a chair. Also used as a decorative detail.

Bracket cornice   A cornice moulding supported by brackets fixed to the frieze.

Bracket foot   A foot supporting a casepiece that is attached directly to the underframing. A bracket foot can be plain, scrolled, or molded. A bracket foot on a bombé piece will outcurve.

Brad   Tiny nail (one inch or shorter) that has little or no head, usually made of brass. Used to attach applied moldings or brasses.

Brass box foot   A squared brass foot, usually castored, often found on eighteenth-century legs of English and American pieces. The French usually favored the metal sabot foot.

Brass inlay   Designs like rosettes, stars, anthemion, and thin strips; made of brass, set into furniture. Examples in Régence period.

Brass shoe   A fitted brass foot terminating in a button or castor.

Brass tacks   Also called brass studs. Examples on Farthingale style chairs.

Breton   A native of Brittany.

Brocade   Any silk material incorporating brocading.

Broken arch pediment   Pediment broken in center of arch.

Broken pediment   A pediment (a pointed or curved piece used above the cornice on tall casepieces) with the moldings broken at the center for ornamental purposes. Greek and Roman temples were the origin. Seen on neo-classical furniture. Highly carved cabinets from sixteenth-century Burgundy were found above broken pediments.

Bronze doré   Bronze mounts. Examples in Louis XV period.

Bronzes d'ameublement   Bronze mounts on furnishings. Examples in Louis XVI period.

Brushing slide   This is a large slide found at the top of some chests. Its purpose was to provide a surface on which the owner's clothes could be brushed. Usually an English element.

Buffet   A sideboard. It is also used to describe open doorless furniture of more than one tier.

Buffet à glissants   Buffet with sliding end panels, having small recessed superstructure.

Buffet crédence   A panelled buffet made in two sections, usually from Provence.

Buffets, Grand or Petite   Similar to English court cupboards. Often in three tiers, the top and middle with drawers. May be large or small. Examples in Louis XIII period.

Bulbous turning   A turned support in which a large bulb-like swelling is featured.

Bun foot   Foot, perhaps of Dutch origin, shaped like a flattened bun. Examples on armoires from Alsace in the eighteenth century.

Bureau   A desk, escritoire, or cabinet.

Bureau à caissons latereaux   A piece of furniture used for writing in the Louis XVI period.

Bureau à cylindre   A cylinder desk with a metal gallery on the top, cabriole legs, often inlaid. Examples in the Louis XV period.

Bureau à dessus brisé   A writing table with a folding top and long tapering legs.

Bureau à pente   A provincial writing piece, narrow, with an oblong top, hinged slant lid.

Bureau plat   A rectilinear table with three drawers in the frieze. The center drawer was recessed. The table was usually veneered and had brass mounts. Examples in Louis XIV period.

Bureau toilette   A table with drawers to hold personal articles. Examples in Louis XVI period.

Burl veneer   The growth, burl, from a tree trunk sliced for veneer. Antique veneer is thicker than new veneers. Many fine pieces with burl veneer were made in the Dauphiné area.

Butt-joint   A joint formed by two pieces of wood united end to end without overlapping.

Button foot   A round turned foot.

Buttoning   Upholstered buttons used to hold heavy upholstery in place. Examples in the Napoleon III period.

"C" and "S" scrolls   Single and double convolutes. Important in the seventeenth century. Also a popular rococo detail during the Louis XV period.

Cabochons   Raised oval ornaments that were used as decorations. They were also called jewels.

Cabriole leg   A leg that curves outward at the knee and inward towards the foot in an "S" shape. This leg is Oriental in origin. Examples on Louis XV furniture.

Cabriolet   A convertible chair back.

Caduceus   Two serpents twining about a rod. Design seen in Régence period. Twined serpent handles popular in Régence period.

Cage work   Any detail that resembles a cage.

Camlet   A material with a ribbed or "watered" effect.

Canapé   A settee, sofa, or couch. Examples in Louis XVI period.

Candle-brackets   Also called "candle-slides." Small sliding platforms built into a casepiece to hold a candlestick.

Candle drawers   Narrow vertical drawers. They are found on either side of the central locker in the interior of various slant-front desks. Also called document drawers.

Cane   Made from stems of palms or grasses that were woven into a mesh. Originated in the Orient as a furniture material. Régence caned beechwood chairs were popular in the second quarter of the eighteenth century.

Canted   Shape resulting when the corners of a square are cut off.

Capital   Projecting piece at the top of a column or pillar.

Caquetoire   A gossip chair. Examples in Louis XVI period.

Carcass   The body of a casepiece. It does not include drawers or doors. It is like a turkey without wings, legs, head or tail.

Card table   Also called a "game table." Usually square or rectangular.

Carlin, Martin   (1730–1785) Master in Paris, 1766.

Carolean   A term for pieces made in the reign of Charles I (1626 to 1649) of England.

Carreau   Large flat cushion. Examples in Louis XVI period.

Carrying handles   Handles on either side of a casepiece to facilitate moving the piece. Examples on medieval chests.

Cartonnier A cabinet on a plinth composed in two sections. The lower section of the cabinet was enclosed; the upper had open, separated shelves. Usually veneered and mounted. Made to stand near a writing table and used for papers. Examples in Louis XVI period.

Cartouche An ornamental scroll design or shield shape. An example is a triple-divided, cartouche-shaped table top in the Louis XV style.

Cartouche-back A chair or sofa back shaped like a cartouche or scroll. An example is Louis XV back rests.

Carved tassels Wood tassels.

Caryatid A sculptural form of a human figure, usually female, used as the top member of a pedestal or as a leg support.

Cast-iron ball-and-claw feet Late nineteenth-century design.

Cast-iron furniture Made in England, on the Continent, and in America. A great amount was designed for gardens and summer houses during the nineteenth century.

Castor Small wheel on a swivel attached to furniture legs.

Cavetto cornice A concave-shaped cornice.

Cellaret A cabinet or stand for wine bottles.

Cellarette drawers Sections of cupboards or buffets with several divisions. Often lead-lined for storage of wine bottles.

Center table A table of various shapes that was often placed in the middle of a hall or a room. An example is an Empire center (centre) table with a lobed marble top on a triangular base.

Central locker This is the storage section in the center of the interior of a slant- or slope-front desk, with the document drawers on either side. Many lockers had secret hiding places behind them where gold coins were often hidden.

Chair seats   Chair seats are approximately fifteen to eighteen inches from the floor. Examples in wood, leather, cane and upholstery.

Chaise à bureau   Small chair for writing table or dressing table, usually caned.

Chaise à capucine   A provincial turned open armchair with a straw or rush seat, stretchered.

Chaise à sel   Wooden chair with a chest under the seat that was used as a salt chest. No arms.

Chaise à vetugadin   Chair without arms similar to a farthingale chair. Introduced in early Jacobean style in the Louis XVI period.

Chaise encoignure   A corner chair. Examples in Louis XV period.

Chaise-longue   A lounge often with cabriole legs, a molded, carved frame and often a buttoned back that was long enough for the sitter's legs to stretch out on.

Challis   Also called challet: a fine worsted wool.

Chamfered   A shaped bevelled edge usually at a forty-five degree angle.

Channel molding   Grooved molding. Examples may be seen on medieval pieces.

Chantourné de lit   A headboard outlined in Baroque "C" scrolls.

Chasing   A type of engraving. Early chasing was done with a pointed metal tool. Examples on medieval mounts.

Chauffeuse A wood chair with a low seat. Examples in Louis XVI period.

Chêne Oak.

Chenille A velvety cord of silk or worsted.

Chequer Squares of contrasting color. Medieval inlay was often in a chequer design.

Chest Storage piece. Medieval box with a hinged lid. Drawers were added in the seventeenth century.

Chest-on-a-frame Raised chest on a frame with legs under it.

Cheval glass A mirror mounted so it can be tilted in a frame, usually full length.

Chevron borders A border consisting of strips meeting at an angle.

Chiffonnier Eighteenth-century piece with several tiers of shallow drawers.

Chiffonière cabinet Cabinets of shallow drawers intended to hold chiffon garments and other flimsy articles.

Chinese bracket feet A squared bracket foot that has a curved inside with flat squared pads.

"Chinese taste" Chinese designs such as pagoda fretwork, including wallpaper with Oriental designs. An eighteenth-century term.

Chinoiserie A style of decoration in which supposedly Chinese motifs are used. Chinoiserie japanned furniture was important in the eighteenth century.

Chintes Indian cottons in exotic colors.

Chintz Originally, any printed cotton fabric. Some chintz fabrics have a glazed surface.

Chip carving A simple low relief form of carving executed with flat chisels and gouges, usually in geometric patterns. This type of carving was done in the medieval period.

Chutes Ormolu decoration in a "V" shape, often in a foliate design. Found on cabriole legs that usually have ormolu sabots (feet). Examples on Louis XV pieces.

Cire perdue Primitive method of making a mold for bronze work.

Classic period Refers to ancient Greece and Rome.

Claw-and-ball foot A dragon or bird claw grasping a ball or pearl. Of Oriental origin.

Claw foot A foot made to resemble that of a lion, dog, or eagle.

Claw table A small table with a circular-shaped top, pedestal, or shaft, and a tripod base with claw feet.

Cloisonne The technique of covering an object's surface with vitrified enamels, separated by metal strips to create a design. Examples seen on table tops in the Near Eastern style late in the nineteenth century.

Clos or mi-clos A bed resembling a high cupboard. Examples from Burgundy.

Closed arch An arch that is not broken.

Cloven hoof feet A split animal hoof. Examples on various Régence center tables.

Club chair A heavily upholstered chair having solid sides and a low back.

Cluster column legs   These are leg columns placed together in a cluster.

Cock beading molding   This is a tiny half circle projecting molding.

Coffer   A medieval chest. The most important piece of furniture in the Middle Ages. It was used as a trunk, a wardrobe, a seat, and even a coffin.

Collar   A round turning. Ormolu collars are found on Directoire commodes.

Colonettes   Small columns. Usually refers to "projecting colonettes" or "partial colonettes."

Columnar support   A support such as a table staff in column form. Examples on Empire mahogany gueridan tables. Circa 1815. These may have marble tops and triangular bases.

Commode   A chest of drawers. A low cabinet usually enclosing shelves or deep drawers. Examples in Louis XVI period with boulle marquetry.

Commode à vantaux   A chest of drawers opened by two doors.

Commode chair   A chair with a deep apron that shelters a chamber pot.

Commode desserts   A commode fitted with drawers and shelves. It has an oblong top and quarter circle shelves at each end.

Compass decoration   Circular, arc, and star designs. Examples on medieval chests.

Concave   A hollow curve; a curve that dips inward. Various eighteenth century casepieces had marble tops with concave sides that followed the shape of the casepiece. Tables may have concave-sided triangular bases such as circa 1830 center tables.

Confidante   An S-shaped sofa for two from the Napoleon III period. One seat usually faced forward and the other backward. Also, a large upholstered sofa with rounded-off ends separated from the larger main section by arms. Examples in Louis XV period.

Console table   Table made in the form of a bracket with its back attached to the wall and its front supported by one or two legs.

Contrasting woods   Woods of different colors. Important for inlay and for marquetry.

Contre-partie   Marquetry tortoise-shell on a brass ground.

Convertible furniture   An outgrowth of railroad and ship furniture. Not to be confused with folding furniture which has a long military history. This was dual purpose furniture.

Convex   A rainbow-shaped curve. A "camel-hump" shaped curve.

Convolute   A scroll or paper-roll shape.

Corbeille de mariage   A Louis XVI-style bridal armoire. Examples found in Normandy.

Corbel   A bracket of slight extent.

Cordonnet   A twisted rope detail. Examples from Liège.

Corner block   A carved block of wood that is employed to strengthen chairs, set at the intersection of seat and legs.

Corner chair   A square-seated chair with its seat placed diagonally so that one corner faces the front.

Corner cupboard Late seventeenth-century cupboard, hanging or free standing, that became fashionable in the eighteenth century. The front is diagonal or curved.

Cornice The horizontal molding at the top of a casepiece.

Cornucopia A horn of plenty. Motif popular on rococo pieces.

Cotter-pin Wires that are clinched on the inside (twisted) of a drawer to hold the handles and plates of a drawer pull. They are easily untwisted to allow brasses to be removed for polishing. Examples in seventeenth century.

Couch A sofa, daybed, or divan.

Country furniture Also called provincial furniture. Furniture made in rural communities of local woods, often primitive, but employing basic designs from the urban areas.

Coquille Shell or scallop design.

Court cupboard A sixteenth-century cupboard. Its upper portion is enclosed and its lower portion is open.

Court work Ornate French, English, and European pieces made for the Crown and aristocracy. America made no similar pieces since they had no court.

Crapaud Tub-shaped easy chair. Examples in Restoration period.

Credenza Sideboard with doors often surmounted by drawers.

Crescent stretcher Stretcher with a semi-circular shape.

Cressent, Charles (1685–1768) Designer in Régence and Louis XV periods.

Crest-rail The top-rail of a furniture back. Crest-rails can be shaped, carved, or both.

Cresting   Ornamental feature added to the uppermost furniture part.

Cretonne   Printed fabric of cotton or linen in all varieties of weaves and finishes.

Crinoline stretcher   A semi-circular stretcher also called a crescent stretcher. Attached to the front legs of a chair and supported by a short member from each back leg.

Crocket   A medieval-style ornament which curves up and away from the supporting surface and returns partially upon itself in a knob-like termination.

Crosier Back   Convex chair back. Examples on Consulate, Directory, and Empire chairs.

Cross-banding   A band or border where the figure of the wood runs across the width.

Cross-hatching   Shallow carving of vertical and horizontal lines imposed on each other. Examples on medieval and provincial chests and chairs.

Cross-laced legs   Detail on eighteenth-century French legs where carved ribbons twist over tapering legs.

Cross-rail   A horizontal bar connecting uprights of a chair back.

Cross-stretcher   X-shaped stretcher. X-stretchers are seen on many rococo tables.

Cross-stretchered seating   Chairs, stools, sofas, settee bases, and Roman curule chairs.

Crotch-grain   Veneer generally cut from the main crotch or fork of a tree.

Cuff   Inlaid or carved bracelet on furniture legs or columns.

Cup   Bottom or base of a turned shaft.

Cup-caster   A wheel or a pivot-mounted roller with a cup that fits over the end of a furniture leg.

Cup-turned   Cup-shaped turning. Curved cup turnings are often used with angular trumpet turnings.

Cupboard   Cabinet for food or clothing. In France it was called an "armoire;" in England it was called an "ambry."

Cupid's bow   The top-rail of a chair back having a double ogee curve resembling a bow. It is called a serpentine top-rail.

Cups   Small, padded finial cushions, often in three graduated sizes, used on bed valances as decoration. The top one might hold a vase with flowers, and bell tassels would adorn each cup. Examples in 1660s.

Curl   A natural figure in wood that resembles a curl.

Curule chair   A neoclassical chair resembling a Roman chair with curved half-circle legs in an "X" shape.

Curule legs   Half-circle legs in an "X" shape. These are also called Grecian cross legs. Examples in Empire period.

Cushion drawer   A drawer set in the upper moulding or frieze of a secretaire or chest having a convex shape.

Cusp   A Gothic detail consisting of a point or knob frequently carved, projecting from the intersection of two curves.

Cut down   A piece whose legs have been shortened or "cut down."

Cylinder fall   The curved, sliding wood top fitted to writing tables or desks.

Cylinder front   A quarter round, fall front of a desk that is either a solid piece or a tambour sliding up and back in quadrantal grooves.

Cyma curve   A continuous curve, half of which is concave and the other half convex. This produces a gentle S shape. An example is the cabriole leg.

Damask   A material of silk, linen or wool with a tough, smooth, shiny surface. Named for the ancient city of Damascus where elaborate floral designs were woven of silk. It is flatter than brocade and reversible.

Daybed   A narrow couch seen from the seventeenth century on. Became large in Empire period.

Decks   Small drawers placed on either side of various chest tops. Examples in Napoleon III period.

Demi-arm   A partial upholstered arm seen on seating pieces. Examples in Louis XV period.

Demi-lune   A half-round shape. Examples on commodes. Also on Louis XVI mahogany card tables with hinged semi-circular tops and square tapering legs.

Dentil molding   Molding that resembles square teeth that need braces because they have space between them.

Desk   A bureau. It has a writing surface, usually with drawers.

Desserte   Furniture of demi-lune shape. Examples in Louis XVI period.

Dessus de marbre   Covered with marble; marble top.

Diamond point   A design usually framed in a rectangular panel consisting of eight elongated pyramids with the four center ones triangular and the four corner ones quadrangular. The diamond point design was sometimes composed of a diamond-shaped pyramid flanked by four small triangular-shaped pyramids.

Diaper Design consisting of diamond shapes in regular repeats. Examples carved on medieval chests; also found on eighteenth-century marquetry pieces.

Directoire French style of the mid-1790s, characterized by an increasing use of Greco-Roman forms and motifs. This is referred to as a neoclassical style.

Dish-top A rounded table top that is dished out flat in the center leaving a rounded, raised edge.

Divan A sofa or upholstered couch without arms or back, originating with the Turkish custom of heaping piles of rugs for reclining.

Document drawer Also called a "document box." A narrow, vertical drawer that is open at the top and is placed next to the central locker in various desk interiors.

Dolphin A marine mammal stylized for furniture design. This motif appears on French, English, and American furniture.

Doreur Gilded, gilt.

Doric column Greek or Roman columns. The Greek ones do not have a base while Roman ones do. They are channeled and have a capital at the top.

Dornix A coarse woolen tapestry used in the sixteenth century.

Double chairs Also called "love-seats." The French term is "confidantes." The English often called them "Darby and Joan seats," and Americans called them "you and me" chairs.

Double feet A double round or double block turning. Examples may be seen on seventeenth-century cane chairs and bannister back chairs.

Dovetail Devices used to fasten wood together by fitting wedge-shaped or dovetail-shaped pieces into corresponding negative spaces. Dovetails exist on ancient Egyptian furniture, proving that "if it works, don't change it." Early ones are not uniform. A lapped dovetail conceals the actual construction.

Dowel Headless wood or iron pin employed for joining two pieces of wood. Dowels are used in place of screws or nails.

Draped torsos Carved draped male figures designed as supports.

Draw-bore process A fifteenth-century device where the pin hole through the tenon was made slightly out of line with those in the mortice walls so that when the dowel pin was driven home, it drew the tenon more tightly.

Draw-runner A device for supporting the drop-lid or fall-front of a desk or secretary. These are also called slides.

Draw table Table which is fitted with leaves; one pulls up at each end.

Drawer blades The wooden strips that separate a drawer into separate sections.

Drawer bottom Lower portion of a drawer.

Dressing table From the seventeenth century. Eighteenth-century dressing tables for men were important.

Dressoir A dresser. Examples in Louis XVI period.

Drop A pendant ornament.

Drop-front   Also called a fall-front. The leaf falls forward and be-comes the writing place; it rests on draw-runners or slides.

Drop-front secrétaire   Examples in mid-eighteenth century, often with a curved rococo silhouette, marquetry, and fine mounts. The lid drops down to form a writing surface.

Drop handle   A pendant mount (hardware) used as a drawer pull. Seen on various seventeenth-century pieces.

Drop-leaf   A table with one or two hinged leaves which can be raised or dropped by bringing swinging legs or supports into position.

Drop ornament   This is an ornament that hangs down, usually from the underframe of a piece. Also called a pendant.

Dropped seat   A seat made concave so that its middle and front are lower than its sides.

Dry rot   When wood shows frailty, cracking, or breaking, produc-ing a gray dry powder. Restoration is a necessity!

Duchesse   A daybed with a gondola-shaped back, often made in three pieces. A Louis XV piece.

Dutch foot   A club foot found on cabriole legs. If a shoe, disc or disk is beneath it, it is called a disc or disk foot. Varieties in-clude a pad, ribbed, snake, or slipper foot. These are usu-ally associated with English and American furniture.

Dwarf bookcase   A small case made after the mid-1800s. It is the height of a table and may revolve.

Eagle heads   Curved C scroll carved eagle heads. If on a center leg, there will be two reversed heads, one on each side of the leg at the uppermost portion. Also seen on arm chairs.

Ear-pieces   The pieces glued at two sides of the top of a cabriole leg. They avoid an abrupt termination at the top of the leg.

Ébéniste   A cabinetmaker. Word derived from ebony which much seventeenth-century furniture was veneered with.

Ebonized wood   Wood stained to look like real ebony. Ash and holly were frequently used for this purpose. Important for inlay. Entire pieces were ebonized in the Régence and Napoleon III periods.

Ebonizing   Close-grained woods stained and polished to resemble real ebony.

Eclecticism   Adapting at will the forms of any previous period.

Edwardian   Pertaining to the reign of Edward VII from 1901 to 1910. Son of Queen Victoria of England.

Egg and dart   A convex molding with a design resembling alternating eggs and darts.

Eglomisé   Decorated glass in which the back is painted or gilded. Named for a French eighteenth-century artist.

Egyptian Revival   Napoleon's 1798 campaign in Egypt and the discovery (seventy years later) of the Rosetta Stone triggered interest in Egyptian designs.

Egyptian taste   A brief attempt to employ Egyptian designs around the turn of the eighteenth and early nineteenth centuries. Napoleon's African campaign, in 1798, brought them to France. English designers also used them to some degree.

Elliptic front   A round front. Examples on Rococo étagères.

Elliptical foot   A circular turned foot.

Embossing   Fabric pressed between engraved rollers with heat to give raised effect.

En carquois   A quiver leg, tapering and fluted, some made to resemble a bundle of arrows or spears crossbound with ribbons. Examples in Louis XVI period.

Encoignures   Corner cupboards.

Endive marquetry   Designs on furniture with patterns resembling flowing arabesque lines. Seen on seventeenth-century tables and chests.

Endive scroll   A carved ornament derived from the endive leaf.

Entre-deux   Elbow-high cupboard with four short legs. In Empire period it has a plinth base.

Escallop   Also called scallop or shell. A flat shell with curved scallops.

Escritoire   A writing desk containing drawer compartments and pigeon holes, with one or more secret ones. The English term secretary (secret) was derived from this word. May also signify a simple writing table.

Escutcheon   A lock plate or shaped piece that covers a keyhole. Can be metal, ivory or wood.

Espagnolettes   Bronze mounts in the form of a Spanish lady. A Spanish mask detail. Examples in Régence period. Examples on Louis XIV commodes in ormolu.

Estamine   An open weave material. In England called Tammy.

Étagères   A series of open shelves. Many examples appear in the Napoleon III period. Some stood in corners.

Extension table   A table which opens from the center and moves in both directions in order to make room for loose leaves in the open part. Contemporary tables are often constructed this way.

Faceted tapering legs   Examples occur in the eighteenth and nineteenth centuries, usually with metal feet.

Fake   A copy of an authentic piece made to be sold as if it were "the real thing," or a piece composed of antique fragments that were not originally together. A fake is a piece made with intent to deceive.

Fall front   Also called a drop-front or slope-front. Various Louis XV secrétaires have a fall-front enclosing a fitted interior with a cupboard below (circa 1775).

Fantasy furniture   A mix of neoclassical designs: nymphs, carved draperies, Chinese mythological creatures, cupids, dragons, blackamoors, mermaids, dolphins, shell chairs, flower chairs, and leaf chairs.

Farthingale chair   Seventeenth-century chair with a broad seat and low back. Originally a woman's chair.

Faun   A legendary demi-god, half goat, half man. Often used as supports on consoles.

Fauteuil   Louis XV-style open armchairs.

Fauteuil crapaud   Chair totally upholstered except for the legs.

Fauteuil à coiffer   Top-rail on a chair back that was bent into a curve so that a lady could lean back and have her hair easily powdered.

Faux bois   Painted finish used to resemble wood.

Feather banding   A border, usually in veneer or marquetry, with two narrow strips laid at opposing angles. Also called herringbone banding.

Felt   Wool, mohair, or mixed fibers pressed into a compact sheet without weaving.

Festoons   Strings or chains carved, inlaid, or painted to resemble ribbons, draperies, foliage, or flowers.

Feuille de chêne   Oak leaf design.

Fielded panels   Raised panels.

Figures   Timber designs, brought out by cutting the wood so that veneers or solid surfaces display various types of irregularities in the grain and in color.

Finger-grip   A groove indented in the lower edge of a drawer-front or on a wooden handle.

Finger-roll   Continuous concave molding in the frame of a piece.

Finial   A decorative ornament that points upward.

Fittings   Metal mounts on furniture.

Flat carving   Also called peasant carving, relief carving, or incised carving. Flat carving can be seen on medieval chests.

Flemish curve   An S scroll. Examples on seventeenth-century cane chairs.

Flip-top table   A card or game table with a hinged top, made in two parts.

Floral-carved moulded frames   Furniture with floral decoration carved on the frame including arms, legs, front rails and crest-rail. The piece, if a chair, may have upholstery on the back and seat. Examples on Louis XV fauteuils that often have cabriole legs.

Floral parquetry Parquetry with flower designs in geometric shapes. Examples on Louis XV and Louis XVI commodes.

Flower head supports Detail where the arm supports are shaped like an open flower into which the arm is attached.

Fluted corners Channels cut into wood or marble top corners. Examples on circa 1780 Louis XVI corner pieces such as encoignures.

Flutes An inlay design resembling the musical instrument. Sometimes the central flute dips below the two side ones.

Fluting A series of rounded convex furrows or channels cut vertically on a column, leg, shaft, pilaster, or canted edge. The opposite of "reeding," which is raised.

Fly rail The swinging bracket which supports a flap or drop leaf.

Foil The point formed by the intersection of two circular arcs. A Gothic detail.

Fondeur A metal caster. A craftsman working at casting metal.

Forme A bench.

Frame The basic skeleton of a piece of furniture.

Free-standing column A column with open space behind it.

French foot A slightly out-turned, rather tall bracket foot that is usually combined with an apron or skirt.

French polish Shellac dissolved in alcohol and water that is applied to a wood surface. Several coats are applied until a hard glossy film covers the surface. May cause the surface of a piece to become cloudy or produce reddish streaks. Introduced into England from France about 1820.

Fret-work   Ornamental work consisting of three dimensional designs within a band or border. They are an applied decoration.

Frieze   A decorative band often found beneath a cornice.

Fringe   Ornamental edging used in upholstering, made of twisted silk or other materials, often with metal.

Fruitwood   Woods such as apple, pear, and cherry. Used for provincial furniture.

Fustian   In the seventeenth century, a material made of cotton and linen. However, some fustians were classed with woolen materials.

Gadroon edges   A decoration resembling almond-shaped reeding or fluting. Popular in the late seventeenth century and the second half of the eighteenth century. Gadroon borders made of ormolu are seen on Louis XVI pieces.

Galbé   Curved outline.

Gallery   An ornamental rail or cresting in wood or metal surrounding the top of a table, desk, or stand. Many examples in the eighteenth century.

Gallon   Narrow binding of cotton, wool, or silk, usually showing fancy weaves.

Games table   See card table.

Garde du vin   A wine cupboard.

Garde-manger   A food cupboard.

Garde-robe   A Louis XV-style armoire from the area around Provence.

Garland   A carved or inlaid floral swag.

Gate-leg-table   Also called a flap-table. A table with fall-leaves supported by folding legs that resemble a gate.

Gâteau   Concentric molding. Examples in Louis XIII period.

Georgian   English period from the accession of George I in 1714 to the death of George IV in 1830.

Gesso   A plaster and glue base for paint or gilt. On japanned pieces gesso was thickly applied under the ground color to give dimension to the chinoiserie designs.

Gilding   Applying a thin layer of gold to furniture. Entire gilded pieces are associated with French, English and other European furniture.

Gimp   Narrow tape of silk or cotton, used for appliqué and for hiding tacks on upholstered furniture.

Glazed   Fitted or set with glass. Examples on secretaries and bookcases.

Glazing bars   Wood strips which frame glass panes. Also known as muntins.

Gothic   The Gothic period was from the thirteenth to the fifteenth centuries. Its main feature was pointed lancet arches. It followed Romanesque designs of the tenth, eleventh, and twelfth centuries.

Gothic revival period   Gothic revival furniture was seen in the early nineteenth century in France, England, and America. Pre-existing Gothic designs were recycled on Napoleon III, English Victorian, and American Victorian pieces.

Gouge carving A type of carving with the designs gouged out with chisels. Examples of gouge carving are seen on early chests.

Grand Siècle Great period.

Grain painting Technique of applying paint to imitate the grain of wood.

Great chairs Throne chairs seen in the fifteenth century in medieval France. Like English Tudor and Stuart wainscot chairs, they were reserved for important people.

Grecian cross-legs Another name for curule legs.

Greek fret Greek key pattern: repeated square hook-shaped forms. Often used as a band decoration.

Greek-key decoration Executed in marquetry on eighteenth-century pieces such as side cabinets.

Griffin A chimerical beast usually having the head and wings of an eagle and the body of a lion. Used as a decorative motif.

Grisaille Grey-painted pieces.

Grooving Incised carving.

Grotesque Describes fantasy in the shaping of forms carved on furniture. Examples on medieval chests.

Guéridon A candle stand from about 1640.

Guild An association of tradespeople or craftsmen.

Guilloche A sixteenth, seventeenth, and eighteenth century design of braided, twisted, or interlaced bands that form interlaced circles. Found on Guilloche friezes, circa 1775, Louis XV transitional pieces, and in Louis XVI period.

Gun-barrel turnings A circular turning that narrows like a canon, usually combined with ring turnings. Examples on table shafts.

"H" stretcher A stretcher in an H shape.

Hair cloth A fabric composed of cotton warps and filling threads of horse hair. Black and very durable.

Half-column A split column set against a flat surface. May also be called a rounded pilaster.

Handhold The end of a chair arm where the hand rests.

Handles Mounts, hardware, pulls, knobs, moving rings or bails, etc.

Herringbone Inlay done with slanting pieces of wood.

Herringbone banding Banding accomplished with slanting pieces of wood. Also called feathered banding.

High chest A high or tall chest of drawers, starting above the feet.

Hipped cabriole leg A leg that outcurves at the top and then straightens out in a slight concave. Examples on Régence pieces.

Holly A hard white wood with a slightly flecked grain that was used for inlay and stringing. When dyed black it was used as a substitute for ebony.

Honeysuckle Ornamental honeysuckle motif derived from the Greeks and often called anthemion.

Hoof feet Horse feet. Seen on French, Italian and English pieces.

Horseshoe back A convex shaped back. Examples on Louis XV and Louis XVI painted fauteuils.

Huchier Medieval craftsman, with limited ability, who constructed chests and primitive cupboards (hutches).

Hunt table A sideboard table without drawers. Also called a hunt board.

Husk A motif resembling a husk of wheat. Sometimes husks were arranged in swags. Examples on provincial pieces.

Icicles Geometric inlays shaped like icicles.

Incised carving Shallow carving. Also called intaglio carving.

Indiennes European printed cottons.

Inlay Inserting wood of a contrasting color or texture into the surface of a piece for decoration. When inlay is done in straight lines it is called stringing. Brass, shell, ivory, pewter, and even straw are also inlay materials.

Inset corner More detailed than a simple notched corner. This corner traces a table top's molded shape. The effect is a contoured pleat.

Intaglio carving Carved incised designs.

Intarsia Inlaid decorative work in which the design is cut out and then placed in corresponding spaces in a veneered or a solid ground.

Invected corner A pinched or indented corner.

Jacob, George Louis XVI period furniture designer.

Jacquard English-Damask tapestries, brocades, and all material with elaborate figures requiring the Jacquard loom.

Japanese lacquer panels Fitted to pieces such as a Louis XV lacquer bureau but originally made in Japan.

Japanese revival   From 1870s to 1910.

Japanning   Lacquering of pieces in the Oriental style.

Jardinière   A flower stand, or receptacle for flowers such as an urn. Ornate table jardinières are seen in Empire designs. These pieces could be four feet in diameter, with divided lead liners, in mahogany with gilt-bronze mounts and supported by animal forms on a wide base.

Jig saw   Saw for cutting pierced or fret work. Originally operated by a treadle. One of the first machines to which power was applied.

Joues   Wings on armchair. Examples in Louis XIV period.

Keystone   A wedge-shaped detail found on crest-rails or arches.

Kite back   A diamond splat.

Klismos   A classic Greek-type chair with a concave back-rail and curved legs. Important in neoclassical designs.

Knee   The outcurved portion of a cabriole leg. It is also called a "hip."

Knob foot   A small round turned foot.

Knobs   Pulls used on drawers and doors of furniture. Also as decoration on machine-made furniture.

Knotted pine   Wood that was originally a second-best plank of timber with rough knots showing. It was used for painted pieces. Today the paint is removed, and these knotted pieces are sold to collectors. Many pieces are fakes produced by persons cashing in on the demand.

La table à manger   Table for eating.

Lacquer   A finish meant to imitate Oriental lacquer.

Lambrequin   A short drapery design.

Laminated wood   Thin layers of wood glued together with the grain of each layer at right angles to that above and below.

Lampas   An East Indian printed silk.

Lancet arch   A pointed arch. Examples on Gothic-style pieces.

Landscape panel   Description of wood grain that moves horizontally.

Lappet   A projecting overlapping carving. Examples found on eighteenth-century cabriole knees resulting in a raised carved edge that lapped over the leg. This is usually an English or American detail.

Lathe-turned   Turning pieces of wood by rotating them against a tool that shapes them. When the term "turned" is used, as in "turned legs," it means lathe-turned.

Leaf scroll mounts   Mounts of ormolu in a leaf design seen on eighteenth-century and early nineteenth-century furniture.

Leaf tip   A design element often found on eighteenth-century pieces with many tips forming a border, often in ormolu.

Les menuisiers   Cabinetworkers.

Les meubles   Furniture.

Les meubles a écrire   Writing furniture.

Les pieds   Legs.

Let-in-top   An expensive detail found on various game tables. The top is slightly recessed (dished) to accommodate velvet, needlework, or leather, allowing it to lay flush with the surrounding wood area. The top "lets in" the additional material.

Library table   A large table, often with drawers or space for books, usually on a pedestal. The name for any flat-top desk used for library purposes.

Linen-fold panel   A design for a panel consisting of a combination of straight moldings in the shape of folds of linen. A Gothic design seen on medieval French, English, Tudor and Jacobean furniture.

Linen press   A frame with a wooden spiral screw for pressing linen between two boards.

Lingère   A Louis XV armoire in the Bordeaux province was often called a lingère.

Lip-molding   Molding that slants downward in a concave curve to a narrow edge. In a cross-section it resembles an upside down thumb. Also called "thumbnail molding."

Liséré   French silk cord fabric made with weft brocaded flowers and warp Jacquard figures.

Lit à colonnes   A bed with four tall posts.

Lit à Turque   Bed with small arched canopy. Examples in Louis XV period.

Lit bateau   Boat-shaped bed.

Lit de repos   Rest beds or day beds. Examples in Louis XIV period.

Livery cupboard   A sixteenth- and seventeenth-century piece with openwork panels or balustered doors for food storage.

Lobe   A rounded projection or shape. Louis XV and Louis XVI pieces often had lobed borders surrounding their marquetry. These borders often combined lobed and angular elements.

Lock plate   Metal piece around a lock protecting a keyhole. Also called an escutcheon.

Locker   The central miniature cupboard in the interior of a desk or secretary.

Looking glass   Mirrored glass. A mirror.

Loose-leaf   Table leaf inserted into the opening of an extension table to enlarge its capacity.

Loose seat   A slip-seat.

Lounge   A late nineteenth-century sofa or couch. Often these pieces had one arm higher than the other.

Love seat   A double chair. A courting chair. "Confidante" and "tête à tête" are French terms. "Darby and Joan seat" is the English term.

Low relief   Usually applies to shallow carving or built-up decoration that does not project far from the surface.

Lozenge   A diamond shape. Examples can be seen on medieval pieces.

Lunette   A semi-circle, half-moon, or fan shape.

Lyre   A decorative design found on classical Greek furniture which used the harp as a motif or detail. The lyre is also one of the most recognizable motifs of the neoclassical period.

Manchette   Armpad. Examples in Louis XVI period.

Maquette   A model of a piece of furniture.

Merchands or Merciers   Dealers in expensive articles and furniture.

Market value   The retail cash value of a piece.

Marquetry   Contrasting inlay. Can be woods alone or combined with tortoise shell, brass and mother-of-pearl. Exquisite marquetry pieces were made for Marie Antoinette.

Marquise   An upholstered armchair with a wide, deep seat. Examples in Louis XV period.

Marquise alcove   A larger corner chair. Examples in Louis XV period.

Married piece   Combined of authentic pieces, but "made-up" from more than one source. Such a piece is not a fake if it is properly identified. Some married pieces are delightful. Some are "hasty weddings," and others are "living-in-sin." An example of a married piece would be a chest combined with an open bookcase.

Mascaron   A mask.

Mask carvings   Motif representing a human face, lion head, or satyr head.

Mask mounts   Ormolu in mask designs. Examples on Louis XV and Louis XVI commode aprons.

Matelasse   A quilted surface.

Mécanicien   A mechanic.

Medallion-back sofa   The center of the curved back has a large circular shape enclosed with a wood frame, with cabriole front legs and canted back ones.

Melon turning   A large round bulbous turning.

Menuisier   A furniture carver.

Meridienne   A short daybed or couch with the arms shaped into the upholstered back creating a slope back.

Mitered joint   A joint cut at an angle, generally forty-five degrees.

Mobilier   Furniture that could be transported or moved. Term used to describe early furniture.

Modillion   An ornamental cantilever beneath the corona or member of a cornice.

Mohair   A woolen material seen in the sixteenth century. In the seventeenth century the term was used in reference to a silk material.

Moire   A fabric with a watered silk appearance.

Molded rims   Rims found on Louix XV pieces often of ormolu.

Moldings   Long, narrow, ornamental surfaces whose profile casts a shadow. Moldings were often enriched with ornamentation.

Monopodium   Classical pedestal support composed of an animal head and a single leg.

Moreen   A coarse wool material used in the late seventeenth and eighteenth centuries.

Moroccan leather   A fine pebble-grained leather made in Morocco from goatskin tanned with sumac. Found on writing tables.

Mortice   A hole or slot made in a piece of furniture that receives a tenon. A construction element that holds two elements together. Found on medieval pieces.

Mosaic work Small pieces of stone forming a design or picture. Examples in Louis XIII period.

Mother-of-Pearl Iridescent inner layer of a shell, usually a nautilus, favored by the Napoleon III period as a decorative inlay for papier-mache. Thin layers of pearl were applied to the surface of a piece, usually in a flower pattern, and japanning was built around this design. Painted decorations and gilding were usually used in conjunction. Also seen on earlier pieces inlaid in wood.

Moucade A wool velvet used in the sixteenth and seventeenth centuries. It came in fancy patterns.

Mounts The handles, escutcheons, and plates seen on furniture. This word applies to iron work, steel work, ormolu, wooden and glass knobs, as well as lock-plates and hinges.

Multiple scooping A round scalloping seen on provincial pieces.

Muntins Strips of wood that separate and hold glass panes in a furniture door.

Napoleon bed Also called an "Empire bed" or "sleigh bed." Has curved ends.

Necking Any small band or moulding near the top of a shaft, pillar or column. May be called a collar.

Needlepoint Patterns hand-worked with a needle using wool or silk, often used in furniture upholstery.

Neoclassic The use of earlier classical forms during the late eighteenth and early nineteenth century.

Neo-Greek The use of classical Greek forms after the original period. Examples in the Régence period.

Nest of tables   Usually four tables that fit together as one or are used separately.

Noyer   Walnut.

Nulling   Another name for gadrooning.

Octagonal top   An eight-sided top.

Oeben, Jean-Francois   (1720–1763) A great furniture designer. Celebrated for his pictorial marquetry. Examples in Louis XV period.

Ogee   A molding with a single or double cyma curve, having an S or double S shape. Bracket feet with a cyma curve are ogee. The ogee curve was developed in 5 B.C. Greek architecture.

Onion foot   A ball-shaped foot. Examples on medieval chests.

Onyx tops   Usually a table top, a translucent quartz, in a milky or grayish color. Seen on eighteenth-century consoles.

Open back   A chair back formed by the framing and splat (or ribs) and not covered with upholstery.

Open talon   A claw-and-ball foot with the claw extending away from the ball.

Ormolu   Ormolu consists of gilded bronze, brass, or copper mounts. Ormolu was an eighteenth-century detail. Very important on Louis XV and Louis XVI furniture.

Orné   Ornate style.

Ottoman   Also called a pouf. A tufted, upholstered seat without arms. This piece became important in the Napoleon III period for seating. It could be rectangular or round. It eventually became an oversized footrest. It was often used in the center of a room. After 1840, it became elaborate. Circular ones might have centers of wood crafting, statuary, lamps, or jardinieres. Also, a canapé or large cushion.

Outrounded corners   The corners of a square or rectangular table-top where a semi-circular curve replaces a right angle. Examples on eighteenth-century bureaus.

Outset canted corners   Corners, usually found on a rectangular top, that are squared and slightly overhung.

Outset rounded corners.   Rounded corners found on a rectangular top and slightly overhung. Examples on Louis XVI bureau plats.

Ovolo   A quarter circle.

Oyster veneer   Concentric circles of various woods for veneer.

Padded arms   An upholstered arm pad on a wood chair arm. Examples on Louis XV fauteuils.

Painted furniture   Furniture with paint rather than stain applied to the surface. Painted furniture has a history reaching back to the pyramids and was practiced in most countries throughout history.

Paired designs   A matched design found on both sides of a piece.

Palmette   A fan or palm motif. Palm leaf associated with Egyptian revival design.

Panel   A piece, usually rectangular, that is sunk or raised from the surface. Panel chests were made in the medieval period.

Panetière   A hanging cupboard for bread. Originated in Southern France. Open frame with turned spindles.

Papier-maché Molded paper pulp that was used for many furniture pieces in the French Napoleon III and English and American Victorian period. It was suitable for japanning and polishing. Many papier-maché pieces were inlaid with pearl and painted with added decorations. Many tilt-top tables were made in this medium. Papier-maché decoration was enhanced around 1825 by the introduction of mother-of-pearl, which was embedded into the varnish before it fully dried.

Parcel gilding An ornamental gilding. Partially gilded or stenciled.

Parisian mounts French ormolu.

Parlor The small salon.

Parquetry Inlay in geometric patterns.

Paterna Oval designs found inlaid on neoclassical furniture.

Patina The mellow quality of color and texture that furniture surfaces, finished or unfinished, acquire with age. Old pieces mellow evenly. If a piece has a glass-like finish, cloudy look, reddish streaks, or all of the above, it is probably French polished. Patinas may not be natural due to chemicals or other unnatural aging effects.

Paw foot Examples on Empire guerdion tables. Originated in ancient Egypt.

Peaked arched scroll A scroll, also called a scoop, having a pointed arch, achieving a tent-like shape. Peaked arch scrolls are found on various scrolled table skirts.

Pedestal table Table with a central pedestal instead of legs. Examples in the Empire period.

Pediment   The ornamental top surmounting a tall casepiece. Some are pointed, some are curved, and some have a broken curve or broken pointed design. On classical Greek or Roman buildings, pediments were triangular.

Peg   A wooden pin or dowel that passes through both parts of a mortice and tenon joint to secure it. Very small wooden pegs were sometimes used instead of nails to join parts of desk interiors including the pigeonhole drawers. Seen on provincial pieces.

Peint   Paint.

Pendant finial   A downward projecting ornament.

Pendant loops   A hanging circular or oval device attached to a small head and varying in width from 3/4 width to 1 inch.

Pied   A foot.

Pied de biche   Scroll foot.

Pieds galbés   Curved feet.

Pier glass   A narrow mirror designed to be hung on a wall between windows, often above a pier or console type table.

Pierced bracket   A lattice-like bracing decoration.

Pierced scrollwork   Carved rococo shapes in serpentine forms (C and S scrolls) that are not solid. Seen on Louis XV consoles with carved leaves and flowers.

Pierced splat   The back splat of a chair in which details of the design are open.

Pietra-Dura work   Panels and table tops composed of semi-precious stones in designs of flowers, birds, shells and arabesques. Examples on Louis XVI chests and in the

Napoleon III and Victorian periods that combined ebony wood, ormolu mouldings, and pietra-dura panels.

Pigeon hole This is an open storage compartment fitted into the interior of a desk. Usually the interior will have document drawers and a central locker as well as pigeon holes for storage.

Pilaster This is a rectangular or half-round column.

Pile Fabric having a surface made of upright ends like fur.

Pillar-and-claw table A table with a center pillar or shaft with three or four outcurving legs.

Pin A hardwood dowel. Associated with provincial pieces.

Pinnacle An upright terminal associated with Gothic designs.

Plank seat A chair seat made from a single piece of wood. Examples on provincial furniture.

Plaques of Sèvres Porcelain plaques made by the Sèvres factory and used to decorate furniture. Examples in the Empire period.

Platform A detail, featuring clustered columns on a flat platform supported by legs.

Platform stretcher The lower shelf of a table. Examples on Louis XV tables with ormolu galleries.

Pliants Folding stools. Examples in Louis XVI period.

Plinth Block, square, rectangular, round, or octagonal piece used as a base of a column or chest when solid to the ground. Circa 1820 side tables often had a plinth base that supported two pairs of columns and a rectangular marble top.

Plush   A fabric, like silk, wool, or cotton, whose pile is more than 1/8 inch high.

Pompeiian legs   American Victorian period, turned Louis XVI style legs that were often decorated with incised carving and applied ornaments, with the largest turning at the top.

Poplin   A silk and worsted material with a corded surface. Early eighteenth century.

Porphyry   A purplish-red stone. Mosaics of porphyry were used on Gothic and Renaissance-style, nineteenth-century pieces.

Pot-board   Open shelf low to the floor on a dresser. Examples seen on provincial pieces.

Pouf   A large Napoleon III or Victorian upholstered stool usually used in the center of a room. A large ottoman.

Première-partie   Marquetry with a tortoise-shell ground and a brass pattern.

Prie-dieu   A chair for kneeling on during prayer, having a high back, a low seat, and a book rest on the top rail.

Primary wood   The wood that comprises the greatest part or outer surface of a piece.

Profile   The side view or outline of an entire piece or an element such as a moulding.

Provenance   A written history or pedigree of a piece. It includes who originally owned it, where it was made, when it was last sold, and so on.

Provincial furniture   Furniture made by regional cabinetmakers from simple farmhouse pieces to fancy bourgeois pieces.

Psyché A cheval dressing glass.

Pull brackets These are located on either side of the top drawer of a desk or secretary and are pulled out to support the writing portion. They may be called desk-slides.

Pulvinated skirt Curved apron with cushion shapes. Examples on provincial pieces.

Punching or punch work Decoration accomplished with a pointed tool in the medieval period.

Putti A motif of a child's head with wings.

Quandrangular baluster supports Legs having four angles and four sides. Examples on Louis XIV giltwood consoles.

Quadrant brackets Quarter-circle cast brass brackets which support the fall-front of a desk or secretary.

Quarter-round pilaster This is one quarter of a circular column. It is often reeded, but can be plain.

Quartering A means of obtaining a formal pattern in wood figure by taking four consecutively cut pieces of veneer that have identical figuring, and setting them in opposing form to achieve a mirrored pattern.

Quatrefoil Four intersecting curves; a four-leaf clover shape. Examples on Gothic pieces in the medieval period and later Gothic-style furniture.

Quilloche carving An ornamental band with paired ribbons or lines that flow in interlaced curves around a series of circular voids.

Quirk The narrow groove at the side of a bead.

Rafraîchissoir   A small table for chilling wine. Top has a metal liner. Examples in Louis XV period.

Rail   A horizontal connecting piece in furniture construction. Chairs have seat-rails, crest-rails (top-rails), back-rails, and stretchers. Rails hold the sides of casepieces together.

Raised edge   This is an important design element found on cabriole legs. The design, usually starting near the seat-rail past the edge of the legs, is a raised layer, plain or decorative, such as carved acanthus leaves. Usually associated with English and American legs.

Rake   The angle or slant of various furniture legs. Examples are seen on rear furniture legs.

Ram's head   Male sheep motif derived from classical origins.

Rattan   Palms of genus calamus. The tough stems used for wickerwork. Often used for bedroom chairs. Wicker has a long history beginning with basket work.

Rayed shell   A geometric half-circle design formed with crisp straight (ray) lines.

Récamier   A daybed with sides of unequal height. The legs are often out-curved. Examples in Directoire period. Named for Madame Récamier.

Récamier sofa   A sofa having raised ends. It is Directoire in design, and was named for Madame Récamier.

Recessed stretcher   A box stretcher with the front rail located a little behind the front legs to allow room for the occupant's heels.

Reeding   A number of narrow, vertical grooves resembling small convex flutings. Examples are seen on many eighteenth-century furniture legs.

Régence style   Style of French furnishings from 1700 to 1720, the period in which a transition occurs from the Baroque style of Louis XIV to the Rococo style of Louix XV.

Regency   Period from 1811 to 1820 during which George, then Prince of Wales, later George IV, was regent of England.

Renaissance   Period in Europe that lasted from the fifteenth to the seventeenth century. A rebirth of art, architecture, and philosophy. Entered France by way of Italy.

Rest bed   Also a daybed.

Restoration   More than repair, restoration means to renew and return a piece to its original state by adding new parts and substituting parts for missing or damaged ones. Restoration is proper and should be respected because without it, many fine pieces would be lost. Good workmanship is very important. Valuable pieces can be ruined by inferior craftsmen.

Riesner, J. H.   (1734–1806) The greatest ébéniste of the Louis XVI period.

Revivals   Designs and styles from previous time periods.

Ribbed ormolu panels   Seen on Louis XVI commodes.

Ribbon-back   A Chippendale chair, with its back composed of twining ribbons. A Rococo design influenced by French rococo styles.

Ribbon-tied sprays   A design carved on arched top-rails often with laurel leaves. An eighteenth-century detail.

Ribs   Usually refers to curved elements.

Rim   Edge around a table top.

Rinceau   An ornamental foliate or floral motif.

Ring and ball   A turning of ring and ball elements.

Ring handles   Examples on Directoire commodes.

Ring turnings   A circular turning. Ring turnings may be composed of one or many rings.

Rocaille   Design of rocks, shells, and plant forms. Examples in the Louis XV period.

Rococo   Elaborate ornamentation with luscious curves that combined shell, rocks, and rustic naturalistic forms. This rather playful style originated in France about 1720. The Louis XV period delighted in rococo forms.

Roe   Dark flakes in a mahogany figure.

Roentgen, David   An eighteenth-century Parisian cabinetmaker noted for his marquetry.

Roll-top desk   A desk that closes by use of a flexible cylindrical hood having a convex shape.

Rolled-arm   Arms having an outward curve or roll, seen on chairs and sofas.

Roman arch   A semicircular arch or a rounded arch.

Romayne   Ornamentation that featured human heads on medallions.

Rope-turned   Turning resembling a rope.

Rosette   Ornament resembling a rose. A circular detail with curved petals.

Rounded fourcorners   Furniture top with four rounded corners. Examples in Louis XVI period.

Round front   Also known as elliptic, swell, or curved front. Examples on various console tables.

Rounded vase turning   Wide vase turning found at top of shaft. Examples on provincial tables.

Roundel   A round desk decorative ornament, sometimes incised. Examples are seen on sixteenth-century pieces.

Runners   Wooden strips attached to the inner sides of a casepiece on which the drawer slides.

Rush seat   A furniture seat made of tightly woven or twisted rush.

"S" scroll   A double-curve scroll. A popular Rococo motif.

Sabots   Decorated metal feet to which casters may be affixed. Usually ormolu. Examples on Régence-period and Louis XV furniture.

Safari chair   A collapsible, portable chair; the legs unscrewed from the frame. This piece was often made of wicker.

Salon   Originally the principal room where the aristocratic or middle-class woman spent much of her time.

Salon sets   A settee and two armchairs in the Louis XVI style.

Satin   One of the basic weave structures in which the filling threads are interlaced with the warp at widely separated intervals, producing the effect of an unbroken surface. Origin Tskinkiang, China.

Satyr masks   Mythological male facial design, often used as ornament.

Sayette Fabric with a twill, diagonal ribbed effect. In England called serge.

Scagliola An imitation stone, from powdered gypsum and glue, that substituted for marble.

Scaling A carving done to resemble fish scales.

Scalloped leaves Serpentine table leaves.

Scalloped top Table top with serpentine edge. Examples on provincial pieces.

Screws A metal fastener with a tapered shank and slotted head. A handmade screw on an original piece fits tightly and is hard to remove.

Scroll back A seventeenth-, eighteenth-, or nineteenth-century chair with scrolled slats. Examples often on provincial pieces.

Scroll foot Also called scrolled toes. A foot which terminates in a tight scrolled form, usually inturning.

Scroll top A curved broken arch pediment used on casepieces.

Scrolled leg Serpentine legs terminating in scrolled feet. Also called cabriole legs.

Scrubbed Condition of pine table-tops that have been worn smooth and are grayish-white in color from years of washing. These were originally kitchen tables.

Secondary wood Wood that is not visible, such as on bracings, backboards, and shelves, and is not the same wood as the one used for the outside or for the principal parts of a piece.

Secrétaire   A two-section writing desk. The lower section is a cupboard; the upper is a dropfront writing table with a fitted interior.

Secrétaire à aballant   A tall upright secretary. Examples in Louis XV period.

Secretary   A desk combined with drawers below, and bookcases or shelves in the upper portion. The upper portion may be closed.

Seigneur   A lord or noble.

Serpentine front   A furniture front having a curve that is convex in the middle and ends, but is concave in between. Louis XV bergères often had a serpentine-fronted seat rail.

Serpentine wing   An upholstered curved arm. Examples on upholstered chairs.

Serre-papiers   A piece that holds papers.

Settee   A light open seat for two to six persons, having a low back and arms. Seen in many styles during many periods.

Sewing table   A small work table. Examples in the seventeenth and eighteenth centuries.

Shaft   A stem, pillar, or column support found on tables.

Shelf   Many French tables have a shelf in their lower portion. Also called a platform stretcher.

Shell design   A seashell design. Examples on Louis XV chairs on their serpentine-front seat-rails.

Shoe   A disk or cushion underneath the foot of a piece of furniture. The term also refers to the piece between the seat-rail and the splat. A chair with the splat and shoe as one piece will usually not be an antique.

Shoulder-pieces The pieces glued at two sides of the top of a cabriole leg. They avoid an abrupt termination at the top of the leg. Also referred to as an ear-piece.

Show-wood The wood that shows on upholstered pieces.

Shuttle lunette A crescent-shaped design found on medieval chests composed of opposing lunettes.

Side-chair A chair that has no arms; in the past, they stood with their backs to the wall when not in use.

Side-table A table designed to stand against (beside) a wall.

Sideboard Usually a dining room piece with shelves and drawers.

Sièges courants Chairs which could be moved at will.

Sièges meublants Chairs that stood against the wall.

Silk Cloth made from the lustrous fiber obtained as a filament from the cocoon of the silk worm. Origin: China.

Skinned A piece that has had its paint removed.

Skirt See apron piece.

Slat-back chair A turned chair with a back of horizontal concave slats. Made from the seventeenth century to the present. A provincial piece.

Sleigh bed Also called a Napoleon bed or an Empire bed. Has curved ends.

Slide A large pull-out shelf on chests for brushing clothes or an additional work area or for writing. Also a small slide to hold a candle. Various Louis XVI tables have a leather-lined slide and a drawer raised on square tapering legs joined by a shelf.

Sliding well   Portion of a slant-top desk interior (usually the center section) that moves or slides out. Designed to conceal a secret well under it for hiding coins or valuables.

Slip covers   Appeared with upholstered furniture.

Slip seat   An upholstered seat that can be removed.

Slipper chair   A chair characterized by a low seat. Usually an upholstered bedroom chair used for putting on slippers.

Slips   The boards that fitted into a circular nineteenth-century dining table when extended to enlarge it. Drawer slips are between the drawer side and drawer bottom.

Sociable   A Napoleon III piece with separate seating sections. Could be two, three, or four parts. Many examples in the Louis XVI style.

Sofa   Developed from the daybed, double chairs and settees.

Spandrel   The space enclosed by two surfaces at right angles, or between an arch and its frame, frequently filled with small fretted ornaments or inlaid fans.

Spider legs   Very thin turned legs.

Spindles   Slender turned pieces of wood.

Spiral fluting   Seen on Louis XVI tapered legs giving a screw effect.

Spiral leg   A leg resembling a twisted rope. Also called a barley or sugar twist of Portuguese or Indian origin.

Spiral turning A twisted turning. Examples in Henri IV period.

Splat The central vertical panel of a chair back. Examples on sixteenth-century wood arm chairs.

Splay leg A leg that flares out.

Spool Turning in the shape of a row of spools. It was used mostly for provincial pieces.

Squab A loose cushion. These were used on medieval seats.

Steel furniture In the eighteenth and nineteenth centuries, steel was often used for folding furniture. Louis XVI had a stationary steel bed decorated with gilt bronze. The Empire period is noted for its steel furniture.

Stem Another name for a shelf, pillar, or column support on a table.

Stile The vertical member in panel furniture. The stile is the outer upright on a piece of furniture.

Stop-fluting Concave fluting alternating with convex fluting. Examples on Louis XV tapered stop-fluted legs.

Straight front A flat front casepiece.

Strapwork Intertwined designs associated with the Renaissance. Examples appear during the reigns of Francois I and Henri II. Also on eighteenth-century Boulle cabinets executed in brass, pewter, and shell on ebony.

Stretcher The crosspiece which connects and braces furniture legs.

Stretcher table A large rectangular table with turned legs joined by rectangular stretchers.

Stringing   Thin bands of inlay for decoration.

Stuff-over chair   One in which the upholstery covers the seat-rails.

Stuffed   Upholstered.

Stuffed seats   Seating pieces with wood frames. May have upholstery on the back, seat, and arms. Examples in Louis XVI period giltwood fauteuils.

Stump foot   Foot which is not a separate portion from the leg, but a slight outward curve which continues directly to the floor.

Subbing   Substituting new pieces on an antique for repairs or deception.

Supporting column   A column at the front corner of a casepiece which supports an overhanging frieze drawer. Examples in the Empire period.

Suspended inlay   Hanging inlay usually attached to a top element such as the top of a leg.

Swan's-neck handle   The brass pull (handle) on a brass plate, with a convex center curve is called a swan's neck, bail, pull, or handle. Usually an English term.

Swell-front   Convex-curved front.

Swelled bracket foot   An outward curved bracket foot. Examples on bombé pieces.

Swing-leg   A hinged leg that supports a drop leaf.

Tabby   A rich, silk fabric with a wavy figure.

Table à fleurs   A table for holding flowers and plants that has a narrow oblong shape fitted with a metal liner. Examples in Louis XVI period.

Table à gradin   A small commode.

Table à ouvrage   Small work table. Examples in Louis XV period.

Table à pupitre   A table for music. A music stand.

Table d'accouchée   A bedside table.

Table à déjeuner   Small moveable meal table for coffee or tea with a marble top, metal galleries and often a median shelf. Examples in Louis XVI period.

Tabouret   A stool.

Tambour   A flexible sliding shutter constructed of thin strips of wood that are glued to a coarse woven backing. Tambour desks were the ancestors of the modern roll-top desks.

Tang   A wire strip of wrought iron bent to attach teardrop and bail handles.

Tapissier   A specialist in tapestry work, wall hangings, and upholstery.

Tassel feet   Resemble dangling ornaments made of thread.

Taupie feet   Thimble or top-shaped feet. Often in ormolu. Examples on Louis XVI commodes.

Tenon   This is a thin projecting piece that fits into a corresponding groove to unite two elements. Construction element found on medieval pieces.

Term figures Term figures are like pedestal terms, except that they display an entire body. They may have feet terminating in a pedestal and are found flanking various Régence cabinets.

Term leg A richly carved and molded tapering pillar leg (may be in human form) with a bold capital. Found on Louis XIV chairs.

Terms Carved male or female busts, minus arms, that terminate in pedestals. Used to decorate uprights.

Tête à tête Two attached Napoleon III chairs positioned for courting, often facing in opposite directions. Some small sofas were also called tête à têtes.

Three-quarter gallery A gallery that surrounds the back, sides, and front corners of a piece. Usually seen on writing tables.

Thumbnail Molding that slants downward in a concave curve to a narrow edge. In a cross section it resembles an upside-down thumb. Also referred to as thumb molding.

Tier tables Small tables with more than two tops arranged one above the other.

Till A covered compartment that was used to store small possessions. Found in various early chests close to the top. They were made of oak or pine on early chests.

Tilt-top table A tripod table with a circular, square, clover-leaf, or octagon top, hinged to tilt vertically. They are seldom shorter than twenty-eight inches.

Tinsel A silk material that had strips of gold thread woven into the ground for sparkle.

Tip-and-turn table Tripod table whose top can rotate as well as tip vertically.

Toe rest   An upholstered pad, for toes, at center of crossed stretchered ladies' desks. Examples in Napoleon III period.

Toilette   A toilet table. Examples in Louis XV period.

Tongue and groove joint   Used for joining two timbers. On one side is a continuous bead-like molding and on the other is a channel into which the bead-like molding fits.

Top-rail   Top horizontal rail of a chair or sofa.

Torchère   Candle stand.

Torse   Figure that stops at the waist.

Torus molding   A bold convex molding.

Tracery   Designs of arcs and circles in intricate patterns. Examples on Gothic-style pieces.

Transitional furniture   Furniture with details from two contiguous periods. This is why it is important to know the major periods and the order in which they appear. The latest characteristics on a piece determine its period.

Tray-top   A table top with a raised molded edge resembling a tray.

Trefoil   A three-arched or fleur de lis shape. Examples on Gothic-style furniture.

Trelliswork   A lattice design. Examples on Louis XIV carved giltwood pieces.

Trestle supports   Rigid frames that support a plank, forming a trestle table.

Trestle table   A table composed of a fixed leaf supported by two or three trestles instead of legs. Trestle tables were simply a wide board placed over trestles that were taken apart when not in use. A medieval or provincial piece.

Triangular base   Examples on Régence tripod tables with a carved stem attached to a triangular base.

Triangular chair   A three-legged chair.

Trictrac table   A game table fitted with a chess board and also a leather gaming surface on the reverse. Can be square or rectangular.

Tricoteuse   Work table with a gallery of metal or wood made to hold spools or balls of wool. Examples in Louis XV period.

Triglyph   An architectural separating device found on Doric friezes. These grooves or half-grooves may appear on Rococo pieces on each side of an astragal-shaped crest-rail.

Tripod table   A table with a pedestal supported by three canted or outcurved legs. Tripod construction is very sure-footed.

Trumeau   A mirror.

Trumpet leg   A turned leg that resembles an upturned trumpet.

Tufting   The tying down of an upholstered surface by means of a button sewed through the upholstery. The arrangement and resulting folds produce a pattern. Examples in Napoleon III period.

Turning   Shaping of wood on a lathe with the help of turning chisels. It was a popular method of decoration during the reign of Louis XIII.

Twist-turning   Double rope or barley twist.

Tympanum arch   The recessed space between the horizontal and the sloping cornice of a pediment.

U-form Found on Napoleon III slipper chairs. The back has a padded U-form with the curved section facing the seat.

Underframe The furniture part that is supported by the legs.

Undulating seat-rail A wavy seat-rail found on Rococo-style sofas with scrolled feet.

Unnatural patina A wood surface showing the result of refinishing, French polishing, or other unnatural devices.

Uprights A vertical member such as a chair stile.

Urn A decorative vase design, usually with a pedestal used as a chair back or as a finial.

Vaisselier horloge Cupboard with a clock.

Valance A skirt, or it can also represent drapery. When it represents drapery, it is often called a lambrequin design or a swag.

Vase-and-ring turned Turning that combines vase and ring shapes.

Veilleuse A daybed.

Veneer A thin layer of wood glued to a base wood. Veneer is also called "thin skin." Used throughout the eighteenth century. Early examples from ancient Egypt.

Venture furniture Furniture made for speculation and sold in places far from origin.

Vernacular furniture Term used to describe furniture imitating high-style pieces with features already out of date.

Vernis Martin Oriental type of varnish developed by the Martin brothers.

Verre églomisé   Method of decorating the underside of a piece with painted gold patterns.

Victorian period   English, 1830–1900; American, 1840–1910; French, 1848–1914.

Vide-poche   A small table for the contents of a gentleman's pockets when he retires. Might contain drawers.

Vitrine   A display cabinet with glazed doors and (often) sides. Examples in Louis XVI period revival styles.

Vitruvian scroll   A repeat of C scrolls creating a wave shape. Examples on eighteenth-century furniture.

Voltaire armchair   A chair with a deep seat, a high upholstered back, padded arms, and short legs. Named for the French philosopher and dramatist.

Volute   A spiral ornamental scroll.

Volute foot   Outward scrolling foot associated with Baroque furniture.

Wainscot furniture   Furniture built with a frame inset with panels. This is architectural furniture. "Wainscot" usually refers to English medieval furniture.

Waisted capitals   Capitals on columns with concave centers resembling a vertical barbell. Examples on Louis XVI pieces such as commodes.

Wall furniture   All furniture designed to stand against a wall. Examples are secretaries, chests, and some chairs.

Wardrobes   A piece of furniture for holding clothes. Developed from the cupboard and cabinet in the late seventeenth century.

Water leaf   An ornamental design derived from a laurel leaf.

Wave design   Seen on cabriole legs on the knee combined with a cabochon on Louis XV chairs.

Weisweiler, Adam   Louis XVI designer.

Wheat ears   An ornamental detail showing several ears of wheat often carved in low relief, high relief, and inlaid.

Wheel back   An oval back with a central paterna or disk, with spokes radiating from the center.

White wood   Natural or unfinished wood.

Whorl foot   A foot carved in the shape of an upcurved scroll. Seen on pieces with French Rococo style.

Winged finials   Urn finials with wings instead of handles, resembling a trophy cup.

Winged monopodia supports   Winged or finned animals, such as dolphins and griffins, or giant wings, featuring one leg. Examples on Empire period tables supported on winged lion monopodia with a mirrored back.

Winged paw   An animal foot with winged carving appearing on its knee.

Wire furniture   Used as garden furniture, plant stands, and serving pieces.

Work table   A table made in the last half of the eighteenth century for women's sewing tools. Some were made of papier-maché. Very expensive ones had Sèvres plaques and metal galleries.

X-form stretcher   Also called a satire. Examples in Régence period.

BIBLIOGRAPHY

The Antiques Directory, Miller, Judith and Martin, Editors, Portland House, New York, 1988.

Art & Decoration Magazine, No. 245, Nov.–Dec. 1983, pp. 96–101.

Art & Decoration Magazine, No. 288, Sept. 1989, pp. 130–134.

Art & Decoration Magazine, No. 263, June–July 1986, pp. 84–89.

Art & Decoration Magazine, No. 299, Jan.–Feb. 1991, pp. 110–114.

Art & Decoration Magazine, No. 299, July–Aug. 1989, pp. 88–93.

Art & Decoration Magazine, No. 300, March 1991, pp. 141–146.

Art & Decoration Magazine, No. 293, April–May 1990, pp. 17–123.

Art & Decoration Magazine, No. 236, Aug.–Sept. 1982, pp. 110–113.

Art & Decoration Magazine, No. 301, April–May 1991, pp. 150–154.

Art & Decoration Magazine, No. 302, June 1991, pp. 125–130.

Art & Decoration Magazine, No. 286, June 1989, pp. 104–109.

Art & Decoration Magazine, No. 285, April–May 1989, pp. 112–118.

Art & Decoration Magazine, No. 270, June 1987, pp. 100–105.

Art & Decoration Magazine, No. 287, July–Aug. 1989–93, p. 88.

Art & Decoration Magazine, No. 284, March 1989, pp. 104–108.

Art & Decoration Magazine, No. 294, June 1990, pp. 117–123.

Art & Decoration Magazine, No. 297, Oct.–Nov. 1990, pp. 140–146.

Art & Decoration Magazine, No. 304, Sept. 1991, pp. 112–118.

Boger, Louise Ade, *The Complete Guide to Furniture Styles,* Charles Scribner's Sons, New York, 1959.

Boorstin, Daniel, *The Creators,* Random House, New York, 1992.

Burckhart, Monica, *Mobilier Louis XVI,* CH. Massen, Paris.

_____ , *Mobilier Régence Louis XV,* CH. Massen, Paris.

Cali, Francois, *Provence—Land of Enchantment.* Rand McNally and Company, Chicago, New York, San Francisco, 1965.

Christie's Auction Catalogue; Important French & Continental Furniture, New York, Thursday, Nov. 1, 1990.

The Complete Encyclopedia of Antiques Compiled by the Connoisseur, L.G.G. Ramsey, Editor, Hawthorn Books, Inc., New York, 1962.

Cuadrada, John, *Architectural Digest,* Nov. 1987, pp. 178–183.

Cuisenier, Jean, *French Folk Art,* Kodansha International, Ltd., Tokyo, New York and San Francisco, 1977.

DeVèze, Lily, *A Brief Guide to French History,* Carcassonne Publishing.

Discovering Antiques, Volume 10, The Story of World Antiques, Freystone Press, New York, Toronto, London, 1973.

Fitzgerald, Oscar, *Three Centuries of American Furniture,* Prentice Hall, Inc., Englewood Cliffs, New Jersey, 1982.

Gonzales, Alvar, *The French Empire Style,* Palacios Hamly Publishing Group Limited, London, New York, Sydney, Toronto, 1966.

Hanour, Hugh, *Cabinet Makers and Furniture Designers,* C. P. Putnamn's Sons, New York, 1969.

Harper Collins Robert French Dictionary, Second Edition, Harper Collins, Glasgow, London, New York, Toronto, 1987.

House & Garden Magazine, July 1989, pp. 55, 94–105.

The Keck Collection catalogue, Sotheby's Auction House, New York, Dec. 5 & 6, 1991.

Knopf, Alfred, *The Lives of the King and Queens of France Duc de Castries,* New York, 1979.

Gairand, Yves Francoise de Perthuis, *Guide du Meuble Régional Preface de Martine Houze,* Editons Hernas, Paris, 1987.

Gasc, Nadine, and Gérard Mabille, *Musées Monuments de France,* Albin Michel, 1991.

L'encyclopédie des Styles, Annie Morand, Editor, Culture, Arts, Loisirs, Marabout, Paris, 1969.

LaCroix, Paul, *France in the Eighteenth Century,* Frederick Ungar Publishing Co., New York, 1963.

————— , *France in the Middle Ages,* Frederick Ungar Publishing Co., New York, 1963.

Longnon, Henri and Francis Huard, *French Provincial Furniture,* Philadelphia and London, J.B. Lippincott Company, 1927.

Maurois, André, *An Illustrated History of France,* The Viking Press, New York, 1957.

Moores, Patricia, *Antique French Furniture,* Patina Press, London, 1952.

The New International Illustrated Encyclopedia of Art, Vol. 9 (French Art & Architecture), General Consultant, Sir John Rothenstein, Gregstane Press, New York, Toronto, London, 1967.

The Nissim De Camondo Museum, Paris.

The Random House Dictionary of the English Language, Jeff Stein, Editor, Random House, New York, 1981.

Sauchal, Genevieve, *French Eighteenth Century Furniture,* G.P. Putnam's Sons, New York, 1961.

Schroeder, Frederick, "Article Dealers, Drawings, the Decorative Arts in Eighteenth Century," *The Magazine Antiques,* pp. 202–213.

Sotheby's Concise Encyclopedia of Furniture, Payne, Christopher, Editor, Harper & Row, New York, 1989.

Tous Les Styles Du Louis XIII Au 1925—Culture, Arts, Loisirs, Paris, 1973, 1980, Sofedis, 1981.

Viaux, Jacqueline, *French Furniture,* C.P. Putnam's Son, New York, 1964.

Winston, Clara and Richard, *Daily Life in the Middle Ages,* American Heritage Publishing Co., Inc., New York 1975.

————— , *The Horizon Book of Daily Life in the Middle Ages,* American Heritage Publishing Co., Inc., New York, 1975.

World Furniture, Riley, Noel, editor, Octopus Books Limited, London, 1980.

Yates, Simon, *An Encyclopedia of Chairs,* The Apple Press, London, England, 1988.

————— , *An Encyclopedia of Tables,* The Apple Press, London, England, 1990.

INDEX